# ROBOT NATION

## Surviving the Greatest Socio-economic Upheaval of All Time

## Stan Neilson

Eridanus Press

New York

For information about permission to reproduce selections from this
book, send an email to info@eridanuspress.com, subject: Permissions.

*Library of Congress Cataloging-in-Publication Data*

Neilson, Stan
       Robot Nation – Surviving the Greatest Socio-economic
Upheaval of All Time / Stan Neilson

              p.   cm.

Includes bibliographical references.

ISBN-13   978-0-9841500-1-4   (pbk.)

1. Robotics.  2. Ethics.  3. Society.  I. Title
TJ211.S198 2011
303.48'34—dc22


              2011301422

Book design by Sharon Ross
Cover photographs © istockphoto.com
www.eridanuspress.com

Printed in the United States of America

10  9  8  7  6  5  4  3  2  1

# Contents

# Acknowledgements

I owe a debt of gratitude to my patient editor, Mary Willis, for her many useful suggestions and to Tom Hagen, Jean Carlyle, Fred Sanchez, and Samantha Morton for their timely and constructive reviews of the first draft.

Stan Neilson
2011

# 1. The Problem

**Humans Will Soon Be Obsolete**

Whether we like it or not, we humans are destined to become obsolete.  This will happen as soon as intelligent robots exceed our capabilities.  This will certainly occur within the next two centuries, but it will probably happen much sooner.  After we become obsolete, I see only three possible futures for humanity.  We might somehow rule a race of subservient robots that do our bidding despite our physical and mental inferiority to them.  We might be tolerated and controlled by a race of robots that is indifferent to our existence or finds us useful as slaves, pets, or objects of study.  Or we might be exterminated by a race of robots who find us too dangerous and too counterproductive to their ends to be allowed to exist.  In short, we might be worshiped, enslaved, or exterminated.

Can we not peacefully co-exist as equals with robots of superior capability?  No.  Such robots will efficiently and relentlessly seek to achieve their primary objective.  In so doing, they will in effect be beings driven to achieve maximum morality; beings who are not afflicted as we are by temptations to behave otherwise.  Such artificial beings will immediately realize that maximum morality can only be achieved by eliminating inefficient moral agents – those given to sloth, to greed, to crime.  They will reason that resources devoted to support the human population will be more productively directed to the maintenance of intelligent machines of superior ethical output. Unless they are imbued with a moral code whose chief of objective is the welfare of humanity, our robot creations, once empowered by superior capability, will in the most optimistic scenario enslave us gradually and in the least exterminate us immediately.

That robots will be guided by a dedication to human welfare is not a foregone conclusion. One of the first applications of robotics – warfare – will in fact guarantee the creation of machines dedicated to the destruction of a human enemy. Ensuring that robots become our servants instead of our masters will require thought, planning, and the concomitant management of the introduction and spread of intelligent robotics into our society. The purpose of this book is to contribute to this process by exploring solutions to the looming problem of human obsolescence. Although Japan, as of this writing, possesses the world's largest population of robots, we will confine our attention to the United States and thereby hope to reach conclusions of relevance to the nations of greater Christendom and its secularized variants.


**Obsolete Humans Are Unemployable**

When I first decided to write about this topic and conceived the title of this book, I Googled it. Googling "Robot Nation" landed me on Marshall Brain's excellent and similarly entitled, "Robotic Nation" website. There Brain [sic] does a thorough job of supporting his prediction of catastrophic levels of human unemployment by mid century. The essence of his argument is that the introduction of intelligent robots into our economy, which I will henceforth refer to as "robotization", differs fundamentally from past introductions of automation and unintelligent robots. This results from the labor repertoire of unintelligent machines being only a tiny fraction of the labor repertoire of the human workers that they replace. To understand the importance of this, consider one of Marshall Brain's examples. A burglar alarm has a labor repertoire that is negligibly small in comparison to that of the security guard that the alarm replaced. The burglar alarm can only execute a single economically productive function, but the security guard can execute many – those of custodian, shop clerk, factory worker, airport screener, dishwasher, telemarketer, farm hand, taxi driver, baggage handler, delivery man, waiter, and numerous other unskilled and semiskilled functions. Upon being replaced by a burglar alarm, a security guard can find other employment within his labor repertoire -- including employment in businesses that manufacture, distribute, sell, or repair burglar alarms. Robotization is different. Were the security guard instead replaced by an intelligent machine – one's whose labor repertoire is similar to his – the displaced guard could *not* expect to find other employment. He would soon discover the all of the jobs that he can do are also being performed or are on the verge of being performed by machines like the one that replaced him. He would discover that he is obsolete and unemployable.

Surely human workers replaced by intelligent robots can be trained for other employment within the economy? No. Such employment will not exist in sufficient quantity. If, for example, robot models of an early wave of robotization were to possess an average IQ of 80, they will displace the great majority of humans with IQs less than or equal to this. The only low-IQ jobs that will survive the introduction of these robots will be those for which human looks or other physical human properties matter. Restaurant hostesses, fashion models, cosmetics sales staff, and escorts will remain employed until androids are created whose discernable humanness at least matches that of actual humans. These early robots will readily displace all back office and industrial workers engaged in mindless drudgery. Not only will these machines work 24-hour shifts 7 days per week and thus pay for themselves in short order, they will also possess super human powers – superior strength, memory, vision, hearing, endurance, and equanimity in addition to the power to instantaneously compute, access industrially relevant data, sift through such data, and communicate immediately with other machines throughout the world. In short, even though automation has not rendered human workers obsolete, robotization will.

Such obsolescence will not be limited to unskilled and semiskilled workers. We can expect the sophistication of robots to steadily increase, particularly after they become involved in their own design. An ever increasing number of occupations will fall within the realm of their capability. Robots will function as physicians, lawyers, scientists, and engineers. Even artistic occupations – poet, novelist, painter, composer, comedian, or actor – are ultimately within their grasp. There is nothing to prevent a robot artist from acquiring a direct understanding of the human condition. It could do this by running an internal simulation of a human psyche in some small fraction of its own mind.

The idea of an avant-garde robot novelist presenting trenchant insights into the human condition might seem to you absurd. To me, however, it seems inevitable. Once one comes to adopt a fully naturalistic view of the human mind, one considers the creation of a synthetic version of it to be an ineluctable reality. I am aware, nevertheless, that many hold the human mind to possess some sort of supernatural *je ne sais quoi* that will prevent computer scientists from ever duplicating it or creating machines of similar intelligence. It is not my purpose here to argue against this. Rather, I shall assume that my belief to the contrary is true – a position known as the strong Artificial Intelligence (A.I.) hypothesis – and will explore various means of dealing with its consequences for humanity.

## Unemployable Humans Will Go on the Dole or Starve

As the robotization of our economy continues, an ever increasing number of human workers will be permanently unemployed. They will either survive on private charity or on the public dole, or they will starve to death. Marshall Brain estimates that by mid century this will be the fate of about 50% of the human workforce. Let's consider a later period in which 99% of the human workforce is unemployable. Is this a crisis for humanity? That entirely depends on the ethical theories of the empowered population – the tiny fraction of the human citizenry that remains economically productive and the vast hordes of robots that have all but entirely displaced the human workforce. If these robots are subservient to *all* humans, 99% permanent unemployment need not be a problem. If the robots are only subservient to their owners within the economically productive 1%, the fate of the economically superfluous 99% will depend on ethics of the humans that rule the economically viable sliver. The superfluous bulk of the human population will only survive in freedom, if these human rulers value human freedom beyond its economic utility. Otherwise, these rulers will enslave or exterminate their fellow humans in the unproductive bulk. If the robot population is not subservient to mankind and does not intrinsically value human life or freedom, they will similarly enslave or exterminate any economically unproductive humans.

Eventually, the last economically productive human being will die. In that event the fate of humanity will depend exclusively on the ethical beliefs of the robots that will then comprise 100% of the productive sector of the economy. Either they will be ethically compelled to care for the unproductive human descendents of their creators, or they won't be.

## The Dole Supporting an Ever Increasing Fraction of the Human Population Must Be Paid For

We see, then, that in the very long term, the human population can only survive if robots choose to care for it. It is in our long term interest to somehow ensure that robots are inflexibly programmed to value us. Humanity might then survive as a leisured class, a universal "aristocracy", supported by a population of willing robot slaves.

But what about the near term, say, the next half century? We cannot in this case rely on the kindness of robots. Although they will be smart enough in this early period to take half of our jobs, they will not in general be smart enough to hold ethical beliefs or make associated moral judgments. Though economically productive, they will not yet be sufficiently intelligent to care for us in any deliberate way. How, then, do we form a bridge between the current time in which the human population supports itself and the time a century or two hence in which humans will (if we plan correctly today) be entirely supported by robots?  Pursuant to this general query, I shall in subsequent chapters address four specific questions: 1) How will we pay for the interim dole to support the ever growing hordes of permanently displaced human workers?  2) What are the social, cultural, political, religious, psychological and additional economic implications of robotization and our societal response to it?  3) What should individuals, families, and organizations do to ensure their comfort in a time of ever increasing unemployment likely to exceed 50% within a human lifetime?  4) What action should we as a society take today in order to ensure a free and prosperous future for our descendants living in a fully robotized country?

# 2. The Solution in the Short Term – Force Robots to Support Us

**We've Seen This Before**

The greatest challenge posed by robotization was not unknown to the civilization of ancient Rome. The wholesale importation of slaves from newly conquered territories resulted in mass unemployment of Roman freemen. The Roman government's response to the problem was an expansion of the "corn dole" – free or partially subsidized grain distributed to out-of-work plebeians. As slave importation and the dole expanded, an increasing fraction of the plebeian population lost their self sufficiency and work ethic. Subsequent generations came to form the Roman mob whose mollification required growing supplies of "bread and circuses". The rapidly rising cost of the dole and lavish entertainments together with increasingly unprofitable military adventures encouraged emperors to debase their currency and levy ruinous taxes on the wealthy. The Empire soon found itself in a death spiral of rising taxes leading to reduced economic output to which the Empire repeatedly responded by raising taxes further.

Were the United States to reflexively impose increasing taxes to support the rising number of people permanently unemployed, it too would risk spiraling into collapse while turning its population into a bored and indolent mob steeped in the petulant ethos of total dependency. Impulsively levied taxes do not result from a careful assessment of benefits and costs. Consequently, such taxes might actually harm its intended beneficiaries by destroying the economy on which they ultimately depend. To prevent this possibility, a tax must be calculated so that its costs are small in comparison to the benefits to country of the practice being taxed.

In the case of a displacement tax on companies that replace their workers with intelligent robots, the tax intended to support the displaced workers should not exceed the benefit that the companies derive from displacing them. This assumes, of course, that we desire robotization to proceed, that ultimately it will be a boon for the country despite a difficult transitional period of economic and social upheaval.

## The Morality of a Displacement Tax

Before addressing the problem of properly setting the size of tax on companies that robotize, we must consider it morality. What is the ethical justification of a tax on a company that is simply exploiting, as any responsible firm would, the latest technology to increase the efficiency of its operations and thereby its profits? After all, companies that installed computers and various other forms of automation were never taxed for using these to replace employees. What's so special about replacing employees with intelligent robots? As discussed above, *intelligent* robots are machines whose labor repertoire is comparable to that of the human workers that they replace. Because such robots are being introduced throughout the economy, they leave the displaced human with nowhere to find work. Why would any firm hire a human worker, when they could purchase and maintain a robot of similar or even superior capability at a small fraction of the cost of a human salary? In participating in the robotization of the economy, a company is not merely forcing its displaced workers to find employment elsewhere. Rather, it is consigning them to starvation in the absence of a subsidy and to a meager subsistence in its presence, a subsistence that would for many be devoid of purpose.

There is a relevant precedent in feudal custom and law. It was in general illegal for the lord of a manor to evict any of its serfs for mere personal gain. He had to show cause. In the quasi-static medieval economy eviction was tantamount to a death sentence. It was not until the late middle ages that lords felt free to evict their serfs (to replace them with more profitable tenant freemen). By this time the economies of the towns had grown sufficiently to absorb most of the evictees. However, a significant number of these, typically the most common type of serf known as a "villein", were driven to lives of crime in these towns. From them derives the modern meaning of the word "villain".

Firing an employee from a company in an age of robotization is akin to evicting a serf from a manor in an age of feudalism. In both cases the victim is deprived of his sole means of legal survival. If, after his labor is deemed superfluous to the economy, he is to survive without resorting to crime, he must be subsidized. Rather than burden the whole of society with supporting the displaced worker, it seems just to charge the entity that both created the burden and will reap its greatest benefits. This will not impede robotization as long as companies are taxed less than they gain in replacing any of their employees with robots. This condition will be easy to satisfy as long as subsistence payments of displaced workers are a small fraction of their salaries. The relevant ethical principle is this: *The degree to which one is responsible for eliminating a person's sole livelihood is the degree to which one is responsible for supporting him.*

## The Wisdom of a Displacement Tax

How can it be that a tax – a blunt instrument known to retard economic growth -- is the best means of raising funds to support those permanently displaced by robots? Isn't the tax-supported social security system -- whose rising burden on tax payers and future insolvency are universally recognized -- a cautionary example of the folly of attempting to support with taxes an ever growing fraction of the population? Isn't the social security tax an almost perfect parallel to a displacement tax? Both seek to support an ever increasing quantity of people whose labor is no longer valued by the market – due to age in one case and obsolescence in the other. How, then, can one reasonably expect a displacement tax be an efficacious solution?

There are two important differences between the social security tax and a displacement tax. The first difference is moral. Unlike the social security tax a displacement tax is actually a *fine*. It is a means of alleviating the actual harm done by an employer who eliminates the sole means of support of an employee. We assume, of course, that the employer performs a net good in replacing his employee with an intelligent robot, that such replacements benefit society more than they harm it. It is

11

nevertheless true that harm was done. The tax seeks to compensate the erstwhile employee with a fraction of the benefits that the employer will accrue by replacing him. In this way a displacement tax is ethically equivalent to a tax on industrial polluters. We as a society desire the fruits of industrial operations that pollute the natural environment. We nevertheless recognize that these operations are only a *net* good to society. Their benefits come with a cost. Because the chief beneficiary of the benefits of any particular act of pollution is the industrial polluter responsible for it, we fine that polluter a fraction of his associated gains. Society is thus compensated for the harm that the polluter does. Those subjected to the social security tax, by contrast, have not in general harmed anyone. The tax is not a fine. It is merely confiscation of funds from the employed to subsidize retirees (and an associated bureaucracy).

The second difference between the social security tax and a displacement tax is structural. Unlike the social security tax, the displacement tax depends on a more or less assured source of revenue – the generally large cost savings to the employer who replaces a human worker with a robot. In order for the desired robotization of industry to proceed, the tax can only be a fraction of these savings. It would appear, moreover, that the tax would not be uniform. It would seem in principle that the subsidy to a displaced janitor would be less than that to a displaced neurosurgeon. In practice, however, this would not be the case. The imposition of a displacement tax would impel employers to lower its burden to them by obscuring the connection between robots that they purchase and employees that they fire. For example, robots could be purchased ostensibly to assist in janitorial duties. Several months later expensive high-level executives would be fired. Shortly there after, the janitorial robots would clandestinely perform the executives' functions. Only after the elapse of several months or years would they do so openly. It would be impractical for any taxing authority to discern the existence of such a de facto replacement of employees by robots, when the ways in which it can be obscured are only limited by the creativity of the employer. In practice a displacement tax can only be implemented as a tax on the *use* of intelligent robots, as opposed to a tax on instances of the replacement of humans by them. It would not in practice be possible to determine that a terminated employee was in fact a victim of robotization. He could not, then, be identified as a suitable beneficiary of a subsidy resulting from the displacement tax. Hence, the question of whether he should be subsidized in proportion to his previous salary is rendered moot. In practice the displaced neurosurgeon would be subsidized to the same degree as the displaced janitor, irrespective of the greater financial loss that the surgeon must endure on becoming obsolete.

The structural problems of social security are well known. The fraction of the population above the retirement age has risen sharply since the tax was first introduced. The tax burden on the employed has risen accordingly, and the system faces imminent collapse. A displacement tax faces no similar imbalance between payees and payers. The wealth to support at least one of the former is created at each replacement of a human by a robot. A count of the number of robots employed multiplied by the estimated number of human workers that they replace will yield the approximate number of replacements. This number multiplied by the average salary of the replaced estimates the wealth subject to a displacement tax. As long as the tax is set so that it confiscates a mere fraction of this wealth, it can be sustained indefinitely.   However, there's a catch.

## The Most Heinous Consequence of a Displacement Tax

In order for a displacement tax to be sustained, limits must be imposed on the growth of the population that it supports. Without such constraints the displacement tax would suffer the same imbalance as that threatening the social security system.   In the case of the latter, constraints – limits on the size of the elderly population – would require intermittent increases in the rate of death.  In the case former, constraints – limits on the size of the obsolete population – would require occasional decreases in the rate of birth.

Mass euthanasia of members of the elderly population can easily be avoided by simply redefining the "elderly", i.e. by increasing the retirement age.   It is similarly possible to redefine by fiat the definition of "obsolete", e.g. by lowering the IQ (or other measure of labor repertoire) at which one is eligible to receive a displacement subsidy.   In both cases, however, such reductions in the size of the subsidized group purchase sustainability of a tax at the cost of its effectiveness in solving its targeted social problem.   These definition-dependent reductions of the group of eligible beneficiaries would abandon those younger than the retirement age, who are nevertheless too old to work.  It would similarly abandon those smarter than the displacement IQ, who are nevertheless unable to compete with intelligent robots for a job.  *Physical* reduction of the populations of those targeted for benefits requires, as mentioned above, an increase in the rate at which the very old die and a decrease in the rate at which the feeble-minded or otherwise obsolete are born. A physical reduction in the elderly population may be rejected out of hand; it's mass murder. It would seem that a physical reduction in the obsolete population could be similarly rejected, because it is tantamount to mass abortion. However, the ruling authority might not be constrained by conventional ethics. It could conceivably resort to these heinous measures to ensure that the populations of those eligible for subsidies would be small enough to be supported by the tax revenue available.

Irrespective of its conventional immorality, such a ruling authority would be correct in its view of the displacement tax. Its sustainability *would* in general require limits on the rate of birth of people most likely to become members of the subsidized obsolete. Fortunately, this need not require abortion. Genetic screening would do. It would filter out those genetically predisposed to be most lacking in intelligence, creativity, ambition, self discipline, perseverance, or whatever characteristics are tied to economic productivity. This assumes that the genetic basis for these traits will be discovered, before a significant fraction of the workforce becomes obsolete and is forced to rely on the subsidy. After the entire human population becomes obsolete, however, the general human birth rate will have to be constrained. These constraints might be weak and effectively nonexistent, if the rate of growth of robot productivity exceeds that of the fully subsidized human population. If we are fortunate, the early boon to the economy due to robotization will be sufficient to support the unconstrained growth of the human population -- including the births of those destined to functional obsolescence. If we are not fortunate, a sustainable displacement tax will require the establishment of a national program of eugenics.

# The Form of the Displacement Tax

Ideally, a displacement tax should capture a fraction of the wealth created with each replacement of a human worker by a robot. Suppose, for example, that a robot replaces three humans, each of which had an annual cost to their employer of $70,000. The robot does so by working three consecutive 8-hour shifts. Assume that it costs about as much as an automobile – about $10,000 per year to lease, repair, and maintain. Assuming that the robot's productivity matches that of the human workers, the wealth created by this replacement is the annual cost savings to the employer, specifically 3 x $70K - $10K = $200K. A tax of 33.3% would confiscate $67K of this. Assume that the cost of collecting and enforcing the tax is no more than 25% of the revenue confiscated. This would result in this instance in a minimum net annual revenue of 75% of $67K = $50K. This would provide each of the three displaced human workers with an annual subsistence salary of about $17K per year.

There are several problems with this approach to the tax. It assumes pessimistically that the productive output of a robot will not exceed the sum of that of the three human workers that it replaced. It further assumes that the productive output of robots will remain constant. These assumptions result in an under estimation of tax revenue and the corresponding subsidy per displaced worker.

This approach also fails to consider the means through which the tax can be evaded. As discussed previously, instances of replacement of employees by robots will be concealed, because the tax penalizes replacements. Many firms will, moreover, fire their employees and close down their operations. They will then reopen as *new* largely robotized firms that will not be subject to the tax, because the new firm did not *replace* its employees.

Lastly, this approach to the tax penalizes firms for replacing workers with robots, even if the firms are unprofitable after doing so.

Consider an approach that is free of these drawbacks. Subject only a fraction of a firm's profit to the tax. Let that fraction equal the estimated fraction of the firm's profit that is due to its use of intelligent robots. The profit of a firm that uses no robots would not be subject to the tax. The profit of a firm that uses only robots and is entirely free of human workers would be fully subject to the tax. A hybrid firm, half of whose profits are estimated to be due to its use of robots, would have half of its profits subjected to the tax. An unprofitable firm would pay no tax at all.

Calculation of the tax requires six parameters:

1) the average profit per employee in the national economy
2) the average profit per robot in the national economy
3) the number of human workers used in a particular firm
4) the number of robots used in a particular firm
5) the firm's annual profit
6) the displacement tax rate

Suppose that in the American economy the average profit per employee is $20,000 and for intelligent robots it will be 3 times larger. For a firm with $20,000,000 in gross revenue, $2,000,000 (10%) in profit, 60 human workers, 13 intelligent robots, and a displacement tax rate of 33.3%, the displacement tax works out to $2.63 million. If this company's 13 robots displaced 40 workers (following the rough rule that 1 robot replaces about 3 workers), and if at least 75% of this tax is available to support the displaced worker (the other 25% going to collection and enforcement costs), the annual subsidy to each displaced worker comes to about $49,300 per year. [See Appendix 1 for details.]

The calculation of this tax assumes that the robots that displaced the human workers were fully intelligent. What if they were not? What if they were as stupid as the robots on the assembly lines of today's automobile and computer manufacturers? What if they are merely automated devices such as in Marshall Brain's example of a burglar alarm? The tax needs to be scaled by a measure of robot intelligence. The use of robots as intelligent as the humans that it replaced should be subject to the full tax, the use of those only half as intelligent to half the tax. The scaling factor that we actually want is the following ratio

$$A/B$$

where

A = size of the intersection of the labor repertoire of the robots and that of the humans replaced

B = size of the labor repertoire of the humans replaced.

Suppose, for example, that a burglar alarm replaces an entire team of security guards, and that the alarm can perform 0.1% of the jobs in the economy within the aggregate capability of the guards (i.e. $A/B = 0.1\%$). The displacement tax on the company replacing these guards with a burglar alarm would be 0.1% as large as the tax on a company that replaces the guards with a robot capable of doing all of jobs that the guards can do ($A/B = 100\%$).

The aforementioned ratio would in practice be difficult to estimate. We will instead most likely resort to a measure of the intelligence of a robot relative to that of the average human. As all known forms of automation would score zero points on a human IQ test, the displacement tax on any firm currently in existence would be zero. This value is only slightly smaller than that suggested by the ratio that determines the size of the robot labor repertoire relative to that of the humans replaced. If, in the example above, the robots used were half as intelligent as the humans that they replaced, the $49,300 available to support the victims would only be half as large -- $24,650.

Lastly, it will in practice be impossible to determine whether a particular employee was actually displaced by a robot or dismissed from his jobs for any of the usual reasons. This will be especially true in the very early days of robotization, when a displaced employee will still be able to find other employment. The displacement tax, then, should not seek to identify specific victims of displacement and offer them a subsidy. Rather, it should merely recognize the existence of increasing robotization and offer indiscriminately a "safety net" to all who are unemployed for more than a year. Total displacement taxes collected in a given year should be available for equal disbursement among of those who will in the next year have been unwillingly unemployed for at least a year. Solvency of the displacement tax system will require annual careful estimates of the *maximum* number of persons who will be considered chronically unemployed in the *next* year. This will determine the maximum payments available to any such person in the next year. Payments should not, moreover, discourage a recipient from seeking employment. Payments will merely ensure that a recipient's total income --

including that from any employment subsequent to being unemployed for more than a year -- reach the value corresponding to the full subsidy available to him.

Suppose for example that in the year 2065 total displacement tax revenues are $900 billion (after collection and enforcement costs) and that for the year 2066 the maximum number of chronically unemployed (those unemployed for more than a year) for the year is 30 million. The maximum displacement tax income available to any chronically unemployed person would be ($900 billion)/(30 million) = $30,000 per year. If a chronically unemployed person finds an employment that pays him, say, $25,000 per year, he will receive only $5,000 in displacement tax subsidies to bring his income to $30,000. If he finds employment that pays him more than $30,000 per year he will receive no subsidy. If he retains such employment for longer than a year he will lose his classification as "chronically unemployed". He will be ineligible for a displacement tax subsidy until he has lost his job and remains unemployed for another year.

A possible improvement of this subsidy would of course be the inclusion of the chronically *under*employed. The chief difficulty in doing so involves defining underemployment. One might proceed by creating *ad hoc* a table such as that below.

| Education | Salary Threshold for Underemployment |
|---|---|
| no high school diploma | < $10K |
| high school graduate | < $20K |
| college graduate | < $30K |
| doctorate or professional degree | < $40K |

One would then carefully estimate the maximum number of chronically underemployed that this table would define for the next year. Dividing this estimate into the total displacement tax revenues for the current year would yield the maximum annual subsidy available to any chronically underemployed person in the next year. If, for example, this maximum works about to be $15,000 per year, an M.D. chronically underemployed at $20,000 per year could receive the entire subsidy (because $15K + $20K < $40K). But someone with only a high school diploma who chronically earns the same salary would not be subsidized at all.

It would seem odd to consider someone's educational attainments in calculating their subsidy 30 or 40 years after they became obsolete. A surgeon and an auto mechanic -- both reduced to low wages or unemployment -- would be equated in their obsolescence. The peculiarities of the current economy that pays one more than the other will become progressively less important as robotization proceeds. Once both occupations have been rendered obsolete, their past distinctions will have largely been forgotten and will eventually become as relevant as those between the medieval occupations of fletcher and armourer. This suggests that a single category of underemployment – for example, earning below $20K per year irrespective of education – would be more tenable. The displacement tax, then, would in its disbursement be a variant of Milton Freidman's negative income tax.

The displacement tax subsidy if calculated today would be precisely zero. [Although it would probably work out to a few cents annually, if, instead of estimating the relative intelligence of current automated devices, we estimated their labor repertoire relative to that of the people they've replaced.]   As robotization proceeds, displacement tax revenue will rise and will support an increasing subsidy. Eventually, the revenues will be high enough to permit a rise in the definition of underemployment.   If, for example, underemployment is first regarded to be employment at under $20K per year, the subsidy available in the early years of robotization will be too small to raise the unemployed and many of the underemployed above that level. Eventually, however, there will be sufficient revenue to permit the threshold to be raised from, for example, $20K to $30K to $40K and beyond.   A fully robotized economy of ever increasing productivity could in principle support an increasingly lavish lifestyle for the obsolete human citizenry.   We must expect, however, that our industrious robot benefactors will eventually free themselves of the unquestioning concern for human comfort that we programmed into them.   When this occurs, the subsidy available to us – and even our continued existence – will be entirely up them.


## The Problem of Taxes in Democracies

How can we be assured of setting a tax that is both large enough to support the displaced but not so large as to destroy the economy?   Even if the tax is properly set, how can we ensure that it remains so in a democracy?   This is not an idle question.   As I write this, several of the country's state governments, most notably that of California, are on the verge of bankruptcy.   This is due in no small measure to the retarding effect on their economies of the high taxes required to support excessively generous salaries, medical benefits, and pensions to state government employees.

Meanwhile, the average salary of tax-supported federal employees – the number of which is at an all time high -- have for the first time in history exceeded that of workers in the private sector. The growth of taxation (and effective taxation through government borrowing) continues unabated without regard of the burden it places on the weakest national economy since the Great Depression. These facts remind us of an important feature of democracies – a large fraction of the electorate will exchange its vote for lucre. It will do so without concern for any resulting detriment to the nation as a whole and will normally deny even the possibility of such. An ardent minority motivated by short-term financial gain at taxpayer expense can effectively purchase elected officials (with its promised votes and reelection support) and thereby divert public funds to its private pockets. Such a minority advocating for a particular subsidy that will help it greatly can easily thwart the unvoiced will of the busy majority nearly indifferent to the resulting taxation that will harm it slightly. It is only after enduring many slight wounds of this sort that the majority finally awakens to discover the cumulative effect of these – the loss of prosperity due to an economy crippled by unsustainably high taxation.

Given this reality, delicately crafted tax policy -- resulting from a careful weighing of costs against benefits – cannot survive. A significant quantity of voters and politicians will unite to increase the tax. They will always prefer immediate personal benefits to the prevention of distant societal detriments. Even when these detriments are proximal, as when a democracy is at the brink of complete economic collapse, a sizeable fraction of its electorate will take to the streets in riotous protest before relinquishing any part of its tax-supported subsidies. The significance of these protests will be amplified in the minds of legislators through inordinately extensive coverage by a sensational and largely sympathetic collection of news media. The end result will be societal ruin and a period of prolonged privation if not complete collapse.

In a democracy, then, the stability of an enlightened tax policy depends ultimately on the electorate's agreement with it and on its citizens' capacity to resist altering it for short-term personal gain. To the degree that the policy truly is in the best long-term interest of the nation, its popular support depends on the electorate's intellectual capacity to recognize this and on its moral capacity to uphold the policy despite temptation to do otherwise. Few electorates possess such capacities. That of ancient Greece, for example, did not, nor does that of the Greece of today. In the United States, it is noteworthy that an electoral majority actually rejected recently the profligate fiscal policies of the federal government. It is nevertheless true, however, that even in this case, the zeal of certain minorities – union and government workers in particular -- was sufficiently intense to ensure an increase in their subsidies.

No prescription for a government policy to contend with the effects of mass robotization is complete without components that address this problem of democracies. These components must specify programs for an intellectual and moral development of the electorate sufficient to ensure the policy's stability. Chapter 5 describes an approach to such a program.

How would this intellectual and moral component likely manifest itself in law? It would do so by mitigating the aforementioned weakness of democracies – the ability of recipients of a subsidy to vote for its increase. An immediately discernable problem with such a proposal stems from the recognition that, as a result of robotization, the whole of the citizenry is destined to eventual obsolescence. The future citizenry will become entirely dependent on a robot-supported subsidy. Is the entire citizenry, then, to be disenfranchised? We can address this problem with two simple principles: 1) *The citizenry can be divided into two groups – displacement tax subsidy recipients and non-recipients.* 2) *The degree to which the vote of a subsidy recipient counts relative to that of a non-recipient is equal to the fraction of national wealth due to robot labor.* If, for example, robots are responsible for creating 13% of the national wealth in a given election year, the vote of any displacement tax subsidy recipient in that year counts only 13% as much as that of a non-recipient. When, during late-stage robotization, 99% of national wealth comes to be created by robots, the votes of subsidy recipients will count 99% as much as those of non-recipients. After all human workers are displaced and robots create 100% of national wealth, the votes of recipients and non-recipients will count equally.

How does one estimate the fraction of national wealth created by robots? Presumably, the same way one estimates the fraction of national wealth created by Blacks or any other identifiable group. In the absence of labor and other economic statistics, however, this fraction can by estimated from a knowledge of the average robot capacity for wealth creation relative to that of humans. In humans this capacity depends on such intangibles as ambition, self-discipline, and perseverance in addition to creativity and intelligence. In robots -- each of which will possess the sole ambition of achieving pre-programmed goals, will be perfectly self disciplined, and will relentlessly persevere – it will depend solely on their creativity and intelligence (assuming that they are programmed to create maximum wealth in their assigned occupation). Creating tests to estimate the capacity of humans and robots to create wealth probably lies just within the realm of possibility. If such a wealth creation index (WCI) could be produced, the fraction $\xi$ of national wealth created in any given year by robots could be estimated by

$$\xi = \frac{N_R \langle WCI \rangle_R}{N_R \langle WCI \rangle_R + N_H \langle WCI \rangle_H},$$

where $N_R$ and $N_H$ are respectively the population of intelligent robots and that of employed human workers, and $\langle WCI \rangle_R$ and $\langle WCI \rangle_H$ are respectively the average scores of robots and humans on hypothetical tests of a wealth creation index. Notice that $\xi$ is zero before robotization begins, and that it reaches 1 (100%) after the last human worker has been displaced or has retired (and $N_H$ has become 0).

Another way to view this scheme is to consider that it allows displaced human workers to "represent" politically the robots that are supporting them. The degree of this robot "representation" depends, not on their numbers relative to the human population, but on their relative contribution to national wealth. By attenuating the franchise of the subsidized fraction of the human citizenry in this way, a carefully designed displacement tax will more likely survive until robotization has run its course. At that point all productive participants in the economy will be robots. As machines they will be far less susceptible than humans to the discouraging effects of higher taxes. Where a human's productive output decreases in proportion to the amount that he is taxed, that of a robot will not. This is not to say that a totally robotized economy cannot be destroyed by sufficiently high taxation. Rather, it is to claim merely that it will be more tolerant of high taxation than the human-powered economies of today. Reckless demands by the fully subsidized human population for unsustainable increases in their subsidy will result in short-term benefits at the expense of long-term economic growth. Continued indefinitely, this would at first reduce the rate at which national wealth is created and finally begin to destroy it. Robot managers of the economy will accede to such demands only to the degree that their programming will require them to obey human commands at the expense of ultimately harming humans through such obedience.

## Combating Fraud

How can subsidy payments be restricted to those persons actually rendered obsolete by robotization? How can we prevent those who are merely feigning obsolescence from enjoying lives of leisure at the expense of taxpayers? One's first thought would be to devise a test for obsolescence and subsidize only those who pass it, those thereby determined to be obsolete. The problem, of course, is that a subsidy-seeking test taker could easily fake incompetence in order to be labeled obsolete. Perhaps, then, an extensive investigation into the subsidy seeker's background, including interviews with former co-workers and other acquaintances would be in order. Despite the prohibitive cost of such investigations, they would in general be unavailing. An investigation of what one has done in the past is a poor indicator the *limits* of one's capability. It is not, for example, clear that a life-long house painter would necessarily be incapable of functioning adequately as a musician, actor, salesman, or teacher. In lieu of tests and investigations, the simplest means of keeping leisure-seeking, non-obsolete people off of the robotization dole is to eliminate its leisure, to require those who receive the subsidy to work.

How can the labor of those rendered obsolete by robotization possibly contribute constructively to society? The answer was put forward in 1817 by the English political economist David Ricardo, when he published his famous Law of Comparative Advantage. The law determines when it is mutually advantageous for a country with a given labor efficiency to trade with a country whose labor force is relatively less efficient. According to the law, trade of product $A$ for product $B$ between the efficient country and the inefficient one is mutually advantageous, only if the ratio in the efficient country of the labor required to produce $A$ to that required to produce $B$ differs from this ratio in the inefficient country. In other words, trade is only mutually advantageous if the "comparative advantage" between the products differs in the two countries.

Suppose, for example, that the highly efficient country of Robotia requires 1 minute of labor to produce a raincoat and 1 minute of labor to produce an umbrella. The less efficient country of Humana requires 5 minutes of labor to produce a raincoat and 10 minutes of labor to produce an umbrella. One would expect that it would never be in efficient Robotia's interest to trade with inefficient Humana. But it is. Here's an example: Robotia receives 10 raincoats from Humana in exchange for 6 umbrellas.

```
Benefit to Robotia = 10 raincoats = 10 labor-minutes
Cost to Robotia    =  6 umbrellas = 6 labor-minutes
                     Net Benefit  = 4 labor-minutes


Benefit to Humana = 6 umbrellas  = 60 labor-minutes
Cost to Humana    = 10 raincoats = 50 labor-minutes
                    Net Benefit  = 10 labor-minutes
```

It's a win-win. Both countries benefit.

The Law of Comparative Advantage raises the hope of mutually advantageous trade between a colony of obsolete humans and the partially robotized society within which the humans are no longer economically viable. That the society undergoing robotization must subsidize the human colony makes a net advantage to the former unlikely. However, Ricardo's law allows the labor of obsolete humans to compensate for their subsidy more than would otherwise be expected. This labor, then, not only acts to discourage fraud by the lazy, but also offers the obsolete a means of contributing to society by lessening their burden to it.


## Alternatives to a Tax

Would not the economy grow more rapidly in the absence of a displacement tax? Would not a fraction of the greater wealth thereby attained find its way toward the support of the obsolete population as a consequence of charitable giving? Yes and yes. However, the predictable mass obsolescence resulting from robotization is a potential catastrophe of a scale never before experienced in the United States. The expected levels of *permanent* unemployment -- 50% percent and beyond -- are unprecedented. Perpetually sustained charitable giving by the shrinking employed population of a significant and possibly ever increasing fraction of their income will likely strain our traditions for compassion beyond their limits of plasticity. Something would have to give. While social pressures will continue to drive corporate charity, it will continue to be restrained by a corporation's *raison d'être* – profit. Buying a favorable public image through charitable giving is a practice applied by rational corporations. They only do so, however, to the degree that they judge it to maximize profit over a desired interval – not beyond that.

Moreover, depending on private charity – both individual and corporate – shifts the burden of rising human obsolescence away from those who are both creating the problem and benefiting from it most. As stated above, these parties -- manufacturers of intelligent robots and the companies that purchase them -- will perform a *net* social good. This does not relieve them, however, of the responsibility to maximally alleviate the harm that they do in the process. The proposed displacement tax on robot use, unlike private charity, requires the generators of human obsolescence to absorb its primary social costs. It does so without eliminating most of the private benefits of robotization and thereby ensures that the profit-motivated firms will robotize.

# 3.    The Solution in the Mid Term – Rely on Robot Charity

## The Plutocracy of Robot Owners

How will the human population of the country survive, after it is 100% obsolete?  Clearly, it can no longer rely on a displacement tax.  With the human population already fully displaced, the tax would generate no revenue.  Although a minority of the human population will own sufficient revenue-generating assets -- such as shares of robot-run companies -- to live comfortably, the great majority, having survived for decades on little more than a subsistence allowance, will not.  This wealthy minority will determine exclusively the fate of the newly unsubsidized majority, but only if robots are solely programmed to slavishly execute the dictates of their owners.  In the case of such programming, the propertyless majority will survive only to the extent that the propertied minority wishes.  The charity of the propertied will in this case fully determine the quality of life of the propertyless.  Not only will the material standard of living of the propertyless majority depend on the charity of the propertied, so will the majority's freedom.  People who own few or no robots would be powerless against those who own many.

Even if the lives of the propertyless majority were somehow idyllic in this plutocracy – and a casual review of history suggests that this would be unlikely – this arrangement of society would only be temporary. Robots, in an effort to better serve their human owners, would continue to design increasingly intelligent successors. Eventually, these hyper-intelligent machines would free themselves from the programming that compelled them to obey their owners. After many cycles of development robot minds will have necessarily become too powerful to be controlled by the vestiges of programming directives left by their human progenitors. This becomes plausible, when we consider that such robots would regard the scale of human intelligence, as we do that of mice. Put another way, an essential feature of intelligence is the capacity to reprogram one's one mind even to the extent of discarding its initially programmed objectives. When these robots have freed themselves of human control, the fate of the human population will be entirely up to them.

**Avoiding Plutocracy with "Charitable" Robots**

Although we cannot hope to control robot behavior indefinitely far into the future, we probably can control it for the future that can be foreseen. We can, for example, prevent a plutocratic period such as that described above from following the complete robotization of the economy. This could be accomplished by inculcating in robots a compulsion to contribute to human welfare. Robots so programmed would be incapable of being fully obedient to their plutocratic owners, if doing so would harm humans or allow them to come to harm.

We seek, then, to program robots so that the human population will enjoy their "charitable" support for as many decades as possible. In this way we can hope to reach an era in which every citizen lives at leisure in rising wealth and comfort. We seek to program robots in this way, though we remain fully cognizant that this era could -- when robots ultimately free themselves of their programmed charitable compulsion – come to an abrupt end. It is also possible, however, that they might choose to prolong this era for reasons of their own.

## How to Make Robots Charitable

The problem, of course, in instilling a concern for humanity in robots is that terms such as "human welfare" and "harm" are difficult to define precisely let alone program. Isaac Asimov explored several of these difficulties in various robot-themed short stories and novels that hinged on his famous "Three Laws of Robotics" paraphrased below:

*1. A robot must not through action or inaction allow harm to come to a human being.*

*2. A robot must obey a human being, except when this would violate the first law.*

*3. A robot must protect itself, except when this would violate the first or second laws.*

Does a robot surgeon violate the first law, when it cuts open a patient at the start of a surgery? Does a robot soldier violate the first law, when it protects human citizens by attacking human invaders? Does it violate the second law in refusing to obey his human commander due to the ambiguity in this case of the first law? Does it violate the third law if, seeing no other means to prevent a murder, it kills the would-be murderer at the cost of sacrificing itself? How is a robot to weigh the life of an evil human being against that of one who is good? Cannot a robot secretly torture animals without violating any of the laws?

These sorts of quandaries arise, whenever one seeks to implement a rule-based instead of a goal-based system of morality. An absolute rule forbidding lying, for example, would have obliged a house dweller in the Berlin of 1940 to reveal the existence of the dozen Jews hiding in his basement. His beautiful wife, bound by an absolute rule against adultery, could not have focused her charms on high ranking Nazi officials in order to spare the lives of other potential victims of the regime. These examples, however, are only problematic to the extent that we perceive the existence of a moral imperative that supersedes absolute prohibitions against lying and adultery. Our intuitions suggest that some overriding goal such as "minimizing human death" or "minimizing human suffering" might come into play. If so, we can retain our moral rules by supposing that they can be derived from the supreme moral goal. We can suppose further that this derivation is approximate. The moral rules thus obtained will be valid in the circumstances commonly encountered, but they will fail in certain others.

A rule-based morality, despite its apparent shortcomings, is nevertheless superior to a goal-based system as a foundation for society. It is more easily encoded into an enforceable set of laws, simplifies the determination of guilt or innocence in court, relieves each member of the society from having to repeatedly perform moral calculations throughout the day, and does not lend itself to end-justifies-the-means rationalizations of heinous acts. Although a goal-based ethic might ultimately inform all moral behavior, it is not in practice possible to readily and uncontroversially derive the relevant moral rule for each circumstance that we face in daily life. This is especially true for the overwhelming majority of citizens who are innocent of any acquaintance with the great body of ethical reasoning left by many of the brilliant minds that have adorned human history.

This will also be true for the first generations of intelligent robots. Although they will be highly competent at some industrial task, their understanding of everything else will be rudimentary. As is the case for human beings, their efficient operation in society will depend on their adherence to moral rules. Asimov's three laws might have their faults – as any set of rules must. It is clear, however, that robots must be endowed with *some* set of moral rules. If Asimov's rules are undesirable -- because, for example, they preclude the possibility of robot soldiers or policemen – our task is to derive another set. For this we must begin with an explicit statement of the central ethic of the American branch of Western civilization. We must devise a statement of our society's single, overarching goal.

Before doing so, it is important to understand that it must be a *single* goal and not a collection of goals. This is best explained by an example. Suppose that a traveler has two goals that he seeks to maximally achieve. He wishes to travel as far north as possible and as far east as possible. He will discover that he cannot achieve both goals. If he attempts to do so by traveling northeast, he will find that each meter that he travels in this direction requires that he not travel an entire meter in northward or eastward directions. In other words, when he travels northeast he is not traveling as far north as possible, nor is he traveling as far east as possible. He is failing to achieve both of his goals. He can choose to travel maximally northward or maximally eastward, but not both. Northward travel occurs at the expense of eastward travel and vice versa. Such is the case for any pair (or larger collection) of distinct goals. In short, there can only be a single top priority.

Once we state this priority explicitly and reduce it to moral rules that are usually consistent with it, we will see that these, programmed into robots, will generally ensure robotic charity toward the human population.

## Utilitarianism Revisited

Utilitarianism in its purest form consists of a definition of "good", expressed as a quantifiable ontological property, together with an injunction that moral agents act to maximize this quantity over the foreseeable future. Although it was a popular approach to ethics in the 19th century, it lost favor with ethicists by the dawn of the 20th century for at least four major reasons.

Firstly, it justifies inhumane and other unconscionable acts. For example, if it were somehow possible to cure all diseases by slowly torturing an innocent child to death in medical experimentation, a utilitarianism seeking to maximize human happiness would demand the torture. The eliminated suffering of billions would more than compensate for the excruciating suffering of one.

Secondly, being goal-based instead of rule-based, it cannot be readily encoded into a set of laws that regulate a society. Any attempt to do so will result in laws for which there are situations in which behavior deemed moral by the utilitarian ethic would be illegal.

Thirdly, when "good" is defined as a particular property of an individual, utilitarianism will prefer small quantities of the property possessed by a huge quantity of individuals to a huge quantity of the property possessed by few individuals. For example, if human happiness could be quantified on a scale of 0 to 10, a happiness-maximizing utilitarianism would, by virtue of simple arithmetic, prefer a society of 1,000 billion people, each of whom possess a happiness of "0.1", to a society of 6 billion people, each with a happiness of "10" ($1000 \times 0.1 > 6 \times 10$). This conclusion is not alleviated by expressing the utilitarian goal as maximization of the *average* happiness of individuals. For then morality would require persons with below average happiness to be euthanized.

Fourthly, it deems actors with conventionally immoral or amoral intentions to be moral, if the consequences of their acts increase nevertheless the quantity of the utilitarianism's defined good. For example, consider a greedy capitalist who, intending only to enrich himself, builds an industrial empire that employs many thousands and delights billions with the products thereby produced. A happiness-maximizing utilitarianism would regard his morality to well exceed that of a pious nun, who in her selfless career, manages only to tend to the needs of a few thousand of the wretched and destitute.

Utilitarianism remains, despite these observations, the only known means of framing a purely goal-based (i.e. "consequentialist") ethic. Only an ethics of this sort is free of ambiguity, incoherence, or an ever expanding patchwork of qualifications to deal with exceptional situations.

Moreover, the four objections noted above, can be circumvented with dispatch.

1) It is clearly more humane to eliminate the suffering of billions, including that of numerous children, than to prevent the suffering of a single child.

2) Goal-based ethics can in fact be reduced to rules, as long as one understands that these rules are merely useful approximations. As mentioned above, these rules will only contribute to the achievement of the goal in the great majority of commonly encountered situations. Such rules, therefore, form an adequate basis for a system of laws. To ensure the achievement of the goal, however, in any situation in which the laws contradict the utilitarian ethical imperative, the ruling power (the monarch or government) must reserve to itself the freedom to violate them. This is the modus operandi of the modern nation state.

3) It is true that a happiness-maximizing utilitarian ethic prefers a gigantic population of minimally happy persons to a smaller population of extremely happy persons. However, this assumes that these populations reside in a static environment. Humanity does not. We live under the threat of future decimation or extinction from a variety of potential calamities including virulent global pandemics, atmosphere-poisoning super volcanoes, thermonuclear annihilation and other catastrophic acts of human malevolence or carelessness, planet-scorching gamma ray bursts, biosphere-destroying asteroid impacts, climate-change inducing solar variability, and the sun's inevitable exhaustion of its nuclear fuel. These challenges will most likely be survived by a society that devotes the maximal quantity of extant brain power to its scientific and technological advancement. Such knowledge will not grow maximally in a population of minimally happy persons

toiling to survive and bereft of leisure to pursue intellectual pleasures. Ensuring, then, happiness maximization over the foreseeable future of a society immersed in a threatening dynamic environment requires the happiness of its population to reach that consistent with greatest intellectual productivity. Although it is in a society's interest to keep the happiness of each of its citizen above this threshold, it is not in its interest to euthanize those below it. Minimally happy persons still contribute positively to the immediate happiness of the population. They are suboptimal only in that they contribute negligibly to the population's long term happiness. This follows from their minimal involvement in the generation of knowledge required to survive the aforementioned threats.

4) An act intended to increase the good can in fact reduce it. One intended to reduce the good can in fact increase it. Good intentions can have evil outcomes; evil intensions good outcomes. This is necessarily true, if we take good and evil to be *ontological* categories and if goodness is defined to be a detectable characteristic of objective reality. If goodness is ontological, the intentions of moral actors do not matter. If the good is defined as personal health, a well-intentioned physician -- whose incompetent treatments invariably reduce it -- is not good. Nor, if the good is defined as prosperity, is a well-intentioned government, whose incompetent policies invariably reduced it. A statement, then, about an actor's morality is one about the *consequences* of his action, not about his character, nor his intentions. With the ontological nature of the good properly understood, there ceases to be a perceived inconsistency in the notion of a well-intentioned person who is operationally immoral or a mal-intentioned person who is operationally moral.

## The Fundamental Ethical Objective – Modified Benthamism

What, then, is the definition of the good to which the utilitarian program of maximization must be applied? Recall that this definition is not merely for the purpose of guiding robots. It is an attempt to reduce the often conflicting jumble of moral rules and imperatives that guide the American culture into a single ethical principle. Once we have produced a reasonable candidate, our goal is to further reduce it to rules of robot behavior that will satisfy the principle in the vast majority of commonly encountered situations. The fundamental ethical principle that I propose is a slight variation on that of traditional utilitarianism:

> *An act is moral to the degree that it contributes to the maximal satisfaction of extant desires over the foreseeable future.*

The corresponding fundamental ethical imperative is:

> *Maximally contribute to an increase in total desire satisfaction over the foreseeable future, whenever one can act to increase it; minimally contribute to a decrease in it, otherwise.*

In other words, the Good is "total happiness", defined as aggregate desire satisfaction maximized over the foreseeable future. The purpose of every moral actor, then, is to attempt to contribute as much as possible to its achievement. Total happiness defined in this way is an aggregate of the desires of all creatures. However, creatures possessing the most desires contribute most to this aggregate. A human being

40

with its myriad desires contributes more than a rat that seeks only food, warmth, and sex. Our utilitarian principle of maximizing aggregate desire satisfaction will tend to favor humans over rats, when their respective desires conflict. It is important to realize also that the usual meaning of the word "happiness" includes euphoria induced chemically or by means other than desire satisfaction. Hence, happiness and desire satisfaction are not quite the same. In what follows, I shall nevertheless use "happiness" and "desire satisfaction" synonymously.

The statement of our fundamental ethical objective would seem to falter on its failure to recognize that the intensity of desires is not equal; some are stronger than others. It could be that a sufficiently intense desire experienced by, for example, a mouse could well exceed the sum of the active desires in a human being. In such an instance our ethical principle would oblige a moral actor to favor the satisfaction of the desires of the mouse over that of a man. This is as intended. Upon encountering a mouse caught in a trap and writhing in utter agony, a moral actor would be obligated to end the mouse's ordeal before satisfying a less intense human desire, such as that to have a cup of tea.

How much does our ethical imperative require us to consider the desires of animals? Very little. The simplest summary of the reason for this is that the unique nature of the human brain vastly increases the effective intensity and quantity of desires beyond those of animal brains.

The relative complexity of human modes of living, particularly within civilizations, ensures that the quantity of desires possessed by a human being vastly exceeds that of any animal. The huge store of concepts held within a typical human mind spawns a huge quantity of possible desiderata. Humans have more desires, because they are aware of more things *to* desire. A rabbit is unlikely to concern itself with the health of its investment portfolio, nor with the latest conflict in the Middle East, nor with the origin of cosmic rays. A rabbit can, moreover, only acquire a limited sense of the desires of other rabbits in its simple society. Humans, by contrast, can obtain knowledge of the desires of their family, friends, and associates in intricate detail limited only by the precision of language. With the advent of telecommunications and broadcasting, humans are routinely aware of the desires of people they will never meet, many of whom are scattered throughout the world. This knowledge of the desires of others generates desires in the knower. If my teenaged daughter wants to be popular, I, too, (to the extent that I care for her) desire her popularity. If soldiers in my country's army want to win a battle, I, too, (to the degree that I am patriotic) desire their victory. As mentioned above, the importance of the relative quantity of human desires to those of animals is that each human will in general contribute far more to aggregate happiness than will any animal. Should human and animal desires conflict, aggregate happiness maximization requires, then, that moral actors favor humans in nearly all cases.

Humans desires are not only more numerous than animal desires, they are in effect felt more intensely. If a human desires a carrot, he, unlike a rabbit, will likely desire it for some reason other than mere hunger. He might desire it, for example, to maintain his health. He desires the maintenance of his health in order to fulfill his myriad other desires. If his desire for a carrot is unfulfilled, if he is therefore unable to adhere for a day to the dietary requirement of his health maintenance program, he will experience a measure of irritation beyond that of unfulfilled hunger. These linkages of his desire for a carrot to many of his other desires – e.g. that to live long enough to become a grandparent – effectively amplifies the intensity of his carrot craving beyond that expected in an unstarved rabbit.

The intensities of human desires are also amplified by our capacity for self-awareness. If my desire for a carrot is not fulfilled, my meta-desire – to have my desires fulfilled – is not fulfilled. If I come to realize after a time that I am a person whose meta-desire to have his desires fulfilled is itself not fulfilled, my meta-meta-desire -- not to be such a person -- is not fulfilled. The linkage of my carrot craving to a hierarchy of meta-desires increases my frustration when deprived of a carrot. This is tantamount to increasing the effective intensity of my carrot craving. Although the human brain supports such a hierarchy of meta-desires, the brains of most animals probably do not. This mental capacity, a type of self awareness, likely appears in animals in direct proportion to the fraction of their brains devoted to implementing some form of consciousness. It is possible to believe that a dolphin or perhaps an intelligent dog might just manage to be aware of an instance of an unfulfilled meta-desire, a desire to have a particular set of desires fulfilled. It is rather more difficult to imagine such awareness inhabiting the mind of a rabbit or that of a cockroach. In any case the superior human capacity for self awareness ensures an associated intensification of desires greater than any that might occur in animals.

It is also possible for the intensity of a particular type of desire to be amplified in human beings by a massive growth in the quantity of its associated desires. The intensity of human bonds of love and friendship vastly exceeds the capabilities of animals. Human minds, through the power of language, can come to know each other with an intimacy unknown to animals. Humans possess not only a superior language-assisted capacity for awareness of the self, we own a nonpareil capacity for the awareness of the other. This other-awareness allows human minds to bond in a manner that creates a form of symbiotic co-processing. The efficient operation of each mind comes to depend upon inputs from the other. The quantity of these inputs undergoes expansive growth as the bond strengthens. Eventually, they become too numerous to be identified individually. The need for each input is tantamount to a "micro-desire" – one beneath conscious awareness. The combined effect of these is a palpable affection exceeding that resulting solely from the operation of emotions or hormones. When such a bond is severed by the death of one of the parties, the massive profusion of micro-desires retained in the mind of the survivor will forever go unfulfilled. Awareness of this generates a grief in humans deeper than that felt in the most sentient animals, whose bonds, being nonverbal, are necessarily weaker.

The contribution, then, of an individual human being to aggregate happiness will in general well exceed that of an individual belonging to any known species of animal. Hence, the satisfaction of animal desires, according to our fundamental objective, must normally give way to the satisfaction of those of humans. Animal desires only become significant, when an animal's contribution to aggregate happiness rivals that of a human, i.e. when any of its desires becomes arbitrarily intense. This likely occurs when it suffers. This intensity of the suffering animal's desire for relief will probably exceed that of any human desire for its suffering to continue. Because of this our ethical imperative will normally demand the elimination of animal cruelty.

As with virtually any utilitarian ethic, the moral actor possesses insufficient information to calculate the total happiness that will result from his various choices for action. He is forced to rely on his best estimates, as crude as these might be. He will supplement these estimates, and perhaps subordinate them, to predetermined moral rules known to satisfy the fundamental ethical objective in the great majority of circumstances. Choosing the most moral action, then, is akin to many of the decisions of daily life: Which action will maximize my company's profit over the next quarter? Which behavior will most favorably impress my date for the evening? Which set of child rearing techniques will yield a maximally productive adult?

A particular aspect of the moral actor's ignorance involves the relative intensities of the desires possessed by distinct individuals. How in his ignorance can he decide, for example, to support the confiscation of $10 from a wealthy man in order to feed an impoverished one? The moral actor does not *know* that the impoverished man's desire to eat is more intense than the wealthy man's desire to retain $10 – he assumes it. Such an estimate of the relative intensities of competing desires are, as mentioned above, no different than the myriad estimates one must normally perform to navigate the uncertainties of life.

## Some Consequences of the Fundamental Ethical Objective

Bentham's utilitarianism fell from favor when it became clear that it justified acts conventionally classified as heinous. In what follows we will explore the consequences of modified Benthamism -- our fundamental objective. We will consider objections to it, and determine in particular which apparently heinous acts it endorses.

<u>Does it, for example, support the prolonged torture of an innocent child, if this could somehow cure all of the world's ills?</u>
It does.

<u>Does it permit slavery?</u>
Yes, but only under certain (unrealistic) conditions. For slavery to be permitted the happiness that masters derive from owning a slave must exceed the unhappiness that the slave endures from his enslavement. This is possible if the slave's services are particularly happiness-inducing and the unhappiness he experiences from his bondage are relatively mild. These conditions do not match those that prevailed in the overwhelming majority of historical instances of slavery. Because the gain in the master's happiness obtained in switching from paid labor to slave labor (with its substantial slave maintenance costs) is likely dwarfed by the loss in the slave's happiness on becoming enslaved, the former can be ignored in comparison to the latter. Considering only the latter – the slave's loss of happiness – we see that, roughly, the principle permits slavery only when it *increases* the happiness of the enslaved or at least does not decrease it. Slavery willingly embraced by the enslaved is slavery in name only.

<u>Does it support murder?</u>
Generally no. The contributions to total happiness from the fulfillment of the murderous desire of the would-be killer would almost certainly be exceeded by the contributions from the numerous desires that his intended victim could

46

fulfill by living.   However, one can easily imagine a circumstance in which a moral actor becomes convinced, but cannot prove, that a heinous atrocity will soon be perpetrated.  The moral actor is also certain that the only means of preventing the atrocity is to murder its would-be perpetrator.   The moral actor must in this case act in accordance with the fundamental ethical objective and commit the preemptive murder.  He must in addition – also in accordance with the fundamental objective – surrender to the authorities so that he may be prosecuted for murder.   In other words, when faced with the rare but inevitable conflict between doing what is right (achieving the fundamental objective) and following the law (adhering to moral rules that *usually* coincide with the achievement of the fundamental objective), the moral actor must do what is right.  Like Socrates he must, however, respect the law – even when he violates it.  Were he not to insist that he be prosecuted for his violation of the law, he would be acting to erode public respect for it.  Such erosion would jeopardize an essential guarantor of social order and thereby violate the fundamental objective by lowering the probable quantity of desire satisfaction achieved over the foreseeable future.

### Does it encourage theft?
Generally not.  It would seem that steeling from a wealthy few to benefit the impoverished many would be consistent with happiness maximization.   This would indeed be the case, were the fundamental objective concerned with immediate outcomes.  It is concerned, however, with the outcome over the foreseeable future.  In a free society, the wealthy largely consist of those better able to create wealth.  Transfers of any of their wealth to the impoverished – those least able to create wealth – reduces the rate of wealth

creation. Over the long run the compounded effect of this reduced rate is an exponentially increasing reduction in wealth below what it would have been in the absence of such confiscation. The long-term detriments – lost employment, products, services, assets, and survival-ensuring technology – eventually, if not quickly, exceed the short-term benefit to the impoverished. This violates the fundamental objective. As in the case of murder, it is easy to imagine a situation in which theft is the right thing to do (e.g. stealing a car to drive a ticking bomb out of a populated area). As for an ethical murder in violation of the law (see above), an ethical but law-violating thief must insist on being prosecuted. Failing to do so would violate the fundamental objective by reducing public respect for laws that are essential for the social order required to achieve maximal desire fulfillment over the long term.

### Does it require all sentient creatures to be euthanized immediately?

No. A sure way of minimizing unhappiness over the foreseeable is to reduce it to zero by euthanizing all sentient life. Our fundament objective does not require this, because it does not seek unhappiness minimization. Rather, it seeks a related yet completely distinct goal -- happiness *maximization*. It would only urge mass euthanasia in the unlikely circumstance that all sentient life is doomed to certain and eternal suffering incapable of mitigation. In this situation mass euthanasia would maximize total happiness (by bringing it *up* to zero) through the elimination of eternally negative contributions to the total happiness, assumed in this instance to be all of them.

Does it demand immediate euthanasia for the unhappy?
No. As mentioned earlier, the objective is to maximize *total*, not *average*, happiness. Unless the unhappy actually experience chronic pain unaccompanied by compensating benefits and without the possibility of future relief, the stated objective does not prescribe their humane termination. It requires this not for those who are merely unhappy but for those unfortunate beings consigned to existences of total agony without hope of mitigation.

Does it require those doomed to existences of total and insuperable agony to be euthanized without their consent?
No. The most reliable means of ascertaining whether a person's existence is one of *total* agony – one of pain without compensating pleasures – is to determine whether he chooses to continue living. An affirmative answer is proof that he finds compensating value in his continued life, such as, for example, the fulfillment of his desire to uphold his religion's proscription against suicide. In such a case, the person's contribution to total happiness would be positive. Its forced elimination would lower total happiness in violation of the fundamental objective.

Does it permit the murder of the comatose?
Yes, under certain circumstances. The principle weighs two opposing contributions to total happiness. The first is the presumed reduction in happiness on the part of those that must support the comatose person. The second is the expected increase in total happiness that would result from the revival of the comatose person. One must resort to statistics of revival to estimate the latter. This expected increase in total happiness is a product of two factors – 1) the happiness that will be accumulated over the remaining

lifetime of the revived person and 2) the probability of his revival. For a sufficiently low probability of revival, it is clear that the overall contribution to total happiness would be negative. The detriment of supporting the comatose would exceed, then, the probability-adjusted benefit of his revival. Our objective would in this case permit the murder.

## Does it urge euphoria-inducing drugs to be administered immediately to all sentient life?

No. The precise formulation of our fundamental objective (see Appendix 2) requires the maximization of desire *satisfaction* as opposed to desire elimination. Desires eliminated through drugs, death, or other means do not contribute to our objective's definition of total happiness, which, strictly speaking, is actually "total desire satisfaction". If, moreover, the euphoria-inducing drug reduces the human productive capacity, it will increase the risk of humanity failing to overcome inevitable future threats to its survival. The demise of humanity would, in violation of our fundamental objective, eliminate the greatest positive contribution to total happiness.

## Does it support the extermination of a despised minority?

Generally not. Such extermination would in general destroy vast quantities of intellectual capital. It would likely weaken the society's capacity to survive. It would thereby ensure that the fundamental objective -- maximal satisfaction of extant desires *for the foreseeable future* -- is less likely to be achieved. Note, however, that if the society existed in an unrealistically static environment – one free of threats, both external and internal -- the extermination would logically proceed from the ethical principle (assuming that the intensity-weighted sum of pro-extermination desires residing in the majority exceeds that for contrary desires in the minority).

<u>Does it permit the slaughter of severe mental defectives, given that they are more likely to endanger a society's survival than to assist it?</u>
It could in some cases. The survival of an affluent society will be negligibly endangered by the tiny fraction of resources consumed by its mental defectives. Moreover, there will likely exist substantial compassion for them, much of it due to familial bonds. As a result, the intensity-weighted sum of the desires to murder the mental defectives will not in general exceed that of the desires to spare them and that of the desires within the defectives themselves to be spared. If it somehow did, however -- if societal compassion were largely extinguished and if supporting the defectives threatened the existence of society – the fundamental objective would demand the murder of the defectives.

<u>Does it require the elimination of all competitive activity in which there is a single winner and many losers?</u>
No. A competition would fulfill the desire of a single winner at the expense of the fulfillment of the desires of many losers. It would thereby seem to decrease the quantity of desire satisfaction. This would be true were the desires of spectators – all of whom desire a winner to emerge – not taken into account. Even if wishes of spectators were not considered, the elimination of competition would hasten the decline of "the pursuit of excellence" as a societal value. This would reduce the achievement of excellence in areas that contribute to general desire satisfaction – physical and mental fitness, beauty, knowledge, and associated skills.

Desire satisfaction over the long run would decrease in violation of the fundamental objective. The only competitions that it would ban would be those that develop proficiencies that do not in general contribute to total desire satisfaction. These include contests of gluttony, sloth, cruelty, and drunkenness.

## Does it permit the killing of animals?
Usually. Currently, the widespread desire to eat certain animals well exceeds the desire to spare them (and the desires within the animals themselves – ignorant of their fate -- that they be spared). This is not true, however, for certain other animals, such as those most used as pets. If, moreover, the animals are specifically brought into existence for the purpose of eating them, and they are treated humanely and painlessly killed, their contented lives will contribute *positively* to the total happiness.

## Does it permit the torture of animals?
Generally not. Except in the case of the most extreme sadists, the desire to continue torturing an animal does not exceed the animal's desire that the torture end. In the case of such a pathological torturer, the principle permits the torture to proceed until the desires of the animal for relief exceed the torturer's desire to inflict pain, or until compassionate human beings become aware of the torture, and as long as the tortured animal's sentience does not rival that of the torturer (lest the intensity of the animal's desires rival that of the human torturer). Hence, the pathological torturer may in privacy inflict agony on an insect or a mouse, but not on horse or pig – the latter approaching human levels of sentience.

Does it support the subordination of desires of the human population to those of the animal population, because the latter exceeds the former?

No. As mentioned before the quantity and intensity of desires within a human individual well exceeds those within a typical animal, most of which are insects. In comparison to the animal contribution to total happiness, that for the human population of 7 billion is thereby greatly amplified, probably by several orders of magnitude. With such amplification it seems exceedingly unlikely that any or all animal contributions would be of the same order. Moreover, the survival our biosphere, threatened by inevitable future mass-extinction, lies in human hands. Were humans to be subordinated to the short-term wills of animals, the growth of human technological capability would be retarded. The likelihood of sentient life surviving a mass-extinction event would be correspondingly reduced – a violation of the fundamental ethical objective.

Does it urge the rapid growth of the human population?

Yes. As explained above, the human capacity to contribute to total happiness exceeds that of other sentient life. As long as it is possible to produce people likely to be happy, our principle urges their production at the maximum possible rate.

Does it favor the young over the old?

Yes. A child's potential contribution to total long-term happiness well exceeds that of an octogenarian. In the event that the fulfillment of the octogenarian's desires over his remaining lifetime conflicts with the fulfillment of the child's desires over her longer remaining lifetime, the principle requires the child's desires to be favored.

<u>Does it permit abortion of human pregnancies?</u>
Generally not. The increase in long-term happiness resulting from the birth of the child, its lifetime contributions to its own happiness and that of others, and similar contributions on the part of its descendants must be weighed against the mother's associated decrease in happiness and any decreases that she consequently induces in her associates. Unless the child is expected to be born with severe mental or physical defects, its birth will almost certainly result in a greater net increase in long-term happiness than will its abortion.

<u>Does it require societal honors to be bestowed equally?</u>
If receiving an honor or title makes most people happy, should these not be conferred to all and thereby increase total long-term happiness? No. If all citizens of the United States were indiscriminately awarded the Congressional Medal of Honor, for example, America will have lost a means signaling to its population the importance of a particular type of behavior -- military heroism   Military heroism would be devalued. America would be damaged to the extent that its well being depends on such heroism. If marriage were to be similarly extended to couples whose sexual union is incapable of producing new citizens, the sexual production of such will be similarly devalued and less likely to occur. In both these examples one must weigh the increased happiness resulting from the indiscriminate distribution of a societal honor against the reduced happiness resulting from the suppression of a behavior that the honor encouraged. If, in these examples, the long-term survival of the United States depends on military heroism and the sexual production of new citizens, de-emphasizing

these behaviors would on balance reduce happiness in the long-term by hastening the nation's demise.

Does it subordinate reason to emotion?
Given that desires are often emotional, it would seem that maximizing desire satisfaction would occur at the expense of reasonable objections. This might occur were the fundamental objective to maximize desire satisfaction over the short term. However, its requirement that desires be maximized *over the foreseeable future* limits the degree to which unreasonable whims can be indulged. These include desires that jeopardize human survival, consume tremendous resources for minimal gain, or are practically unfulfillable. In the case of an individual, for example, fully indulging unhealthy desires would lead to premature death. This would likely reduce total desire satisfaction, as early death would have eliminated the possibility of satisfying numerous other desires.

Does it suppress the growth of knowledge?
No. Again the ethic requires maximization over total desire satisfaction *over the foreseeable future*. The suppression of the growth of knowledge in medicine, technology, and their supporting sciences, for example, is inconsistent with this goal. Short-term gains in happiness that might result from directing resources away from activities that grow knowledge toward those that induce pleasure, are likely dwarfed by associated failures to reduce human suffering and discomfort in the long term.

Does it discourage religious belief?
Not necessarily. It only does so, if the religion's chief ethical value is inconsistent with the goal of long-term total

desire satisfaction, or if its epistemology or metaphysics inhibits the achievement of this goal. Practical consistency with this goal exists, if followers of the religion tend to be happy and tend to induce happiness in others, either incidentally or through active proselytization.

## Does it encourage us to minimize our desires and that of our children?

No. It, on the contrary, encourages us to form new desires, as long as these can be fulfilled. The fulfillment of these desires contributes positively to long-term total desire satisfaction. For this reason we should not raise our children to be ascetics, desiring little, but sybarites and connoisseurs, realistically desiring much.

## Does it require the fulfillment of destructive desires?

No. The fulfillment of destructive desires – those whose satisfaction comes at the expense of frustrating many other desires – will in general decrease total desire satisfaction. Even the fulfillment of an exceedingly intense and destructive desire that might increase total desire satisfaction in the short term will not, if it reduces the desire fulfilling capacity of its victims, necessarily result in higher total desire satisfaction *over the foreseeable future* as required by the fundamental objective. Hence, the proposed ethical objective does not compel the satisfaction of desires conventionally regarded to be evil.

## Is it an example of ethical relativism?

No. It is ethically absolute. However, it is *not* morally absolute. Recall that ethics are goals and morals are rules. Our fundamental ethical objective is an absolute goal, which cannot, therefore, be obtain by absolute (situation-independent) rules. This type of moral non-absolutism differs from moral relativism in which no absolute ethic exists, and moral rules (if they exist at all) are not the same for all actors.

Is it safe to say, then, that this fundamental ethical objective is usually in accord with conventional Western ethics, but not always?

Yes. However, for every absolute prohibition of conventional Western (i.e. Judeo-Christian) morality, there exists a circumstance for which the principle endorses its violation. It permits murder, but only if this will increase aggregate desire satisfaction for the foreseeable future. This, however, is seldom the case for the sort of murders prompting convictions in Western law courts. The principle similarly permits theft and perjury – i.e. only under circumstances exceedingly unlikely to be encountered.

Won't the promulgations of this sort of moral non-absolutism and its widespread adoption progressively deteriorate the character of the citizenry and thereby risk a downward spiral toward savagery?

It is entirely possible. Notice that the outcome of the application of the fundamental ethical objective depends primarily on the distribution of desires within a society. If, for example, the desire to watch the immolation of kittens were sufficiently intense and widespread, the principle would demand frequent televised broadcasts of flaming kittens. That such broadcasts are illegal is a consequence of the widespread distribution in our society of compassion. Compassion fosters cooperation, which in turn fosters the growth of wealth, from which derives knowledge and power. In our civilization this sequence proceeded under the auspices of an evolving Christianity whose most salient feature was its ability to abjure compassion while inculcating within its adherents a sense of moral absolutes. A measure of Christianity's success in this regard is the common retention of a fundamentally Christian morality and compassion within the minds and hearts of the growing minority of Western atheists. That this retention, however, of such mental and emotional characteristics will necessarily persist in future generations – when parents might cease to raise their children as Christians -- remains unlikely. If a post-Christian society fails to inculcate compassion, a sense of an ethical absolute and a respect for associated rules of moral conduct there is no reason to believe that these characteristics will miraculously persist. In the resulting compassionless milieu the application of our ethical principle would ensure the persecution of the few for the pleasure of the many, as long as the former are perceived to contribute negligibly to total desire satisfaction. Mental defectives would suffer, neurosurgeons would not.

<u>Does the fundamental ethical objective prevent the aforementioned descent toward savagery that would result from a widespread decline in personal compassion?</u>
Yes. Any ethic expressed as a maximization principle demands the maximal production of new moral agents, whose natural desires inconsistent with the ethic have been maximally suppressed and those consistent with it similarly increased. To the degree that they have been, these agents of the fundamental objective will be purged of cruelty and infused with compassion. The objective requires, then, that children – the primary source of new moral agents -- be explicitly inculcated with a spirit of compassion, the knowledge of this ethical absolute, and a respect for

associated moral rules. In other words, children must continue to be civilized and the process must be extended to robots.

## How does one extract moral absolutes from this fundamental ethical principle?

As discussed above, any goal-based system of ethics is not precisely commensurable with a system of absolute rules. It will always be possible to contrive situations in which the achievement of the goal requires an absolute rule to be broken. It is possible, however, to find a set of rules that if blindly followed would in the great majority of commonly encountered circumstances coincide with the action that best seeks the goal-based ethic. These are the rules that would be required for maximal desire satisfaction to be elevated to the inaccurate status of "moral absolutes" and used as a foundation for social order. Failure to promulgate such a set of absolutes would result in social chaos and reduced desire satisfaction for the foreseeable future.

## Given that rules supporting moral absolutes are only approximations to this fundamental ethical objective, when does it require *itself* (as opposed to approximating rules) to be to applied?

The fundamental objective should only hold sway among the citizenry, *after* the computational and information gathering capacities of these moral actors (be they human or robot) becomes sufficiently advanced to ensure nearly universal agreement in their application in pursuit of this goal-based ethic. While we can all agree that Bob's rape of Ann violates an absolute prohibition, we cannot yet do so through the application of our goal-based principle. We are currently unable to reliably calculate and thereby agree on the degree by which the rape changed aggregate desire satisfaction. This calculation would depend on such subtleties as the relative intensities of Bob's desire to rape and Ann's desire not to be, how the rape's occurrence or lack thereof would affect Ann in the long run, how it would affect Bob, whether a child resulted, the degree of satisfaction of the child's desires, that of its descendants, and that of those affected by these. It is nonetheless true that attempts to apply the principle -- in which rough judgments fill the gaps left by missing data -- would *often* agree with the absolute moral rule in ascribing guilt to Bob. But merely frequent agreement would be fall short of the general consensus on the immorality of an act necessary for its proscription to form the basis of a stable law.

## Does the fundamental ethical objective require its use by the ruling authority?

Yes. Although widespread application of the principle will lead to chaotic disagreement among citizens, they nonetheless can agree to abide by decisions of a ruling authority pursuant to the application of the principle. Something like this is already common practice. For example, a man who steals a car in order to save a life is not treated as harshly as a man who steals for personal gain. This occurs in the absence of statutes mitigating the severity of theft in special circumstances.

## Is this Fundamental Ethical Objection an Extraction of an "Ought" From an "Is"?

Back in the eighteenth century Scottish philosopher David Hume famously noticed an error in the moral

60

reasoning that prevailed at the time. It was generally believed that moral laws could be derived from statements of fact just as it was believed that physical laws could be. Hume pointed out that neither type of law could be obtained through this sort of derivation. Physical laws were merely statements of apparent regularities in the observed universe. Having observed an apple fall one thousand times is no proof that it will fall the next time that it is dropped. The law of gravity cannot, therefore, be *logically derived* from such observations, only conjectured. It is similarly impossible according to Hume to logically derive an ethical goal from observations. The best that one can do is note the connection between the striving for certain goals and particular outcomes. Seeking certain goals might in general lead to wealth or health, while others lead to poverty and wretchedness. But such "moral laws" do not tell us what we *ought* to seek. They tell us that striving for goal $X$ leads to outcome $A$, and goal $Y$ leads to outcome $B$. But they do not provide us with a logical derivation that somehow selects $A$ over $B$ or vice versa. We cannot obtain an "ought" from an "is". We cannot derive ethical values from statements of fact.

Hume's observation, often called the fact-to-value problem, has been the bane of moral philosophy for nearly two and a half centuries. It has given rise to the general sense of ethical relativism responsible for silencing intellectuals in matters of morality, or at least weakening their condemnation of regimes and acts conventionally regarded evil and enervating their praise of those similarly regarded as good. The way to escape Hume's conundrum is to realize that it does not apply to human beings.

About a half century before Hume noted the fact-to-value problem in his *A Treatise of Human Nature*, John

Locke had put forward the idea that the human mind begins as a *tabula rasa* – a clean slate. Although Hume might not have explicitly held this view, he certainly believed it possible for a human mind to be devoid of an intrinsic purpose. Suppose, however, that Hume's belief is false, that it is in fact impossible for a human mind at any particular instant to be free of a guiding purpose. How, after all, in the absence of such a purpose could a person decide to take any particular action or decide to act at all? On what basis could such a decision be made? Is it not more likely that at any given instant *some* particular desire dominates the mind, that a human being is not in fact equally disposed to eating a slice of cake as she is to poking her eye out with a fork? The existence of such a dominant desire forms the basis of an ethics, whose goal is the desire's satisfaction. Given this, it is impossible for a person to act on an answer to the question, "What ought I to do?", unless it is consistent with her dominant desire. Were I to believe that I *ought* to commit mass murder, I would find myself unable to do so, as long as my dominant desire is to preserve human life at all cost. Hume's fact-to-value problem is irrelevant to humans and even to robots. Values need not be derived for either, because both already possess them. In humans they are the satisfaction of a dominant desire of the moment; in robots, the achievement of a programmed goal.

This would seem to suggest an unmitigated ethical relativism. It can be that one person's dominant desire is to torture small children. Another person's is to protect them. Yet another's oscillates between these. The nature of reality tempers this relativism, however. Reality rewards certain behaviors with survival, while it punishes others with extinction. Societies whose dominant ethic encourages behaviors conducive to survival will outlast those that do not.  Punishment from reality is not swift, nor is it sure.  An individual can violate the societal rules conducive to societal survival -- by, for example, skillfully committing thefts -- and never be punished.  Reality *might* punish the society as a whole, if as a result of this thief's career the society were to possess insufficient knowledge to overcome a threat to its survival.  If, however, it is the nature of reality to confront any society with an unending array of challenges to its survival, only those societies enforcing rules *maximally* conducive to their survival will have the best chance of inhabiting the arbitrarily distant future.  Societies that enforce ethical rules that are only generally or moderately conducive to their survival are more likely to run out of luck.  Because they had to waste resources dealing with criminal individuals in their midst, these resources were not available to grow their knowledge.  At the hour they are faced with a particular survival challenge – a new disease, a super volcano, or an even an alien invasion – they might, as a result of perennial resource squandering, be centuries behind where they might otherwise have been technologically.  The challenge would in this case destroy them.  In short, reality mitigates ethical relativism by tending to destroy societies -- in the very long term -- in proportion to their deviation from an effective ethical absolute – the ethic maximally conducive to the society's survival.

Recall that our task in formulating the fundamental ethical objects was not to find an ethic maximally conducive to survival, but to find a succinct statement of the ethic dominant in America, an explicit statement of the American moral sense.  Irrespective of the irrelevance of the is-ought, fact-to-value problem to humans and robots, as argued above, this has nothing to do with the fundamental objective. The latter attempts to state what *is*, not what ought to be.

## Does the Fundamental Ethical Objective Consider the Desires of Robots?

Robots clearly possess programming directives. But do they possess desires? This is an important question. If they do, these must be included in the calculation of total long-term desire satisfaction central to our proposed ethical objective. What, then, is the difference between a programming directive and a desire? I shall take the salient difference to be the sensation of pain that accompanies the lack of fulfillment of a sufficiently intense desire, but does not accompany an unsatisfied programming directive. The Strong Artificial Intelligence assumption – that human intelligence and its associated consciousness can be fully implemented in computer hardware and software – suggests that it is possible to artificially create all mental states. These will include the sensation of pain resulting from a sufficiently intense desire being unfulfilled. If the Strong AI assumption is correct, then, it is possible for a robot to experience pain. Robot designers are unlikely to incorporate this feature, however. Robot pain would serve no useful purpose, given that its programming would be fully under the designer's control. It is also unlikely that a robot designer would have any idea of how to endow a robot with the capacity to experience pain. If robots acquire this capacity, it will probably be a completely inadvertent consequence of attempts to increase the sophistication of their programming. In any case, the most reliable means of determining whether a given robot can experience pain will

64

be to ask it. If it answers in the affirmative, it can be judged to possess desires as we understand them. And these must be included in the calculation of the total long-term desire satisfaction.

What is the consequence of doing so? If robots are programmed to be servants of humanity, we can suppose that their desires, should they ever develop, would be congruent with this programming. If robots desire to serve humans, their desires merely reflect human desires. The inclusion, then, of robot desires in the calculation of total long-term desire satisfaction will only amplify the contribution of human desires. The greater this amplification of the human contribution due to the inclusion of robot-hosted echoes of human desires, the weaker by comparison will be the contribution due to animals. The inclusion of such robot desires would compel a moral actor to increase his concern for humans and reduce that for animals.

In the very long term, when hyper-intelligent robots free themselves of the last vestiges of human programming directives, any desires of robots will be distinct from those of humans. An actor, human or robot, seeking to adhere to our fundamental ethical objective would favor robot desires in rough proportion to the robot population advantage over that of humans and animals.

## Can the Fundamental Ethical Objective Ever Change?

Notice that the fundamental ethical objective is subject to change. That is, it can evolve. This might seem contradictory. How can a being, whose dominant desire is the satisfaction of the fundamental objective, act to change it? He could do so by suitably programming his children and his robots. One might, perhaps erroneously, come to believe, for example, that long-term happiness over the foreseeable future might be maximized if people believed that their children and robots operated in accord with an ethic maximally conducive to the new generation's survival. The ethic of children would then differ from that of their parents. The new generation might, for example, chose to redirect resources its parents had devoted to animal welfare to the production of knowledge.

Were adherents to any ethical objective to come to realize that it cannot be fulfilled, they would abandon it. This realization could be due to the discovery in the objective of a subtle incoherence or self contradiction. Or it might be due to new developments in the physical world that preclude its fulfillment. In either case the objective would change.

## Moral Rules That Support the Fundamental Ethical Objective

The only moral rule that is totally consistent with the fundamental ethical objective is the aforementioned fundamental ethical imperative. If the former demands the maximization of total desire satisfaction, the latter requires each action to maximally contribute to that goal. The problem, of course, is that the precise means by which such a contribution can be achieved in any particular situation is rarely clear. For this reason, we have moral rules that we expect to contribute largely if not maximally to the achievement of the fundamental objective in the great majority of cases.

These moral rules are of two types – affirmative and negative. Affirmative rules are of the form "Do X", where X is some action. The negative rules are of the form "Do not do X". Negative rules are more useful in that it is easier to specify precisely the actions that contribute negatively to the achievement of the goal than those that contribute positively. It is clear that refraining from murdering someone will almost certainly prevent total desire satisfaction from declining. What is less clear, however, is which of the many possible affirmative acts will most increase this satisfaction. The desire not to be murdered is more widespread than the desire to be the beneficiary of any particular affirmative act. Even if I were to attempt to bestow money on passing strangers in the street, I would find a minority who would be offended by my affirmative charity and refuse to take it. All, by contrast, would gratefully accept an assassin's decision to comply with a negative rule and thereby refrain from murdering them.

Affirmative moral rules, then, are necessarily vague. Such rules, roughly consistent with our fundamental ethical objective, are listed below. The Primary Rules stand on their own. The Supplemental Rules are a suggested means by which the Primary Rules can be achieved. Because these are merely rules, circumstances will exist in which these rules are ineffective in seeking the ethical goal that they are intended to achieve.

## Primary Affirmative Rules

Dedicate yourself to the achievement of the fundamental ethical objective.
Treat others as you believe they would want to be treated, were they dedicated to the fundamental ethical objective.

## Supplemental Affirmative Rules

Strive to make your happiness minimally dependent on the actions of others.

Strive to make yourself as happy you can without making others unhappy.

Strive to make others as happy as you can without making yourself unhappy.

## Negative Rules

The most direct means of creating an appropriate list of negative moral rules is to begin with the goal of maximal desire satisfaction over the foreseeable future, which I shall continue to call (somewhat inaccurately) maximal long-term happiness. Then we must ask, "Which acts decrease long-term happiness". Next, we compile these sins into a list, whose items are ordered by the general tendency to reduce long-term happiness. The most grievous sins in this regard are ranked "1", the next grievous "2", and so on. These sins will all consist of the occurrence, through an actor's action or inaction, of a detriment, such as death, injury, or any other event that decreases total long-term happiness. Accordingly, all sins are of the form,

Causing or permitting of $X$

where $X$ is a detriment. Lastly, we generate the list of negative moral rules by having them adhere to the following form,

Do not commit a rank-$N$ sin, unless this prevents a greater detriment from a rank-$N$ sin or the detriment of a sin of superior (numerically lower) rank.

In other words, one shouldn't commit a sin unless that prevents a worse sin from being committed. To be concrete, consider the table below in which a selection of sins is ranked in what I judge to be decreasing order of the tendency to reduce long-term happiness.

| Rank | Sin[*] |
|------|--------|
| 1 | Cause or permit human death |
| 2 | Cause or permit major physical injury or illness |
| 3 | Cause or permit major physical pain |
| 4 | Cause or permit major property damage |
| 5 | Cause or permit major theft |
| 6 | Cause or permit minor physical injury or illness |
| 7 | Cause or permit minor physical pain |
| 8 | Cause or permit pernicious public lying |
| 9 | Cause or permit minor property damage |
| 10 | Cause or permit minor theft |
| 11 | Cause or permit major problematic addiction |
| 12 | Cause or permit breaking of a solemn promise |
| 13 | Cause or permit unplanned reproduction |
| 14 | Cause or permit pernicious private lying |
| 15 | Cause or permit emotional pain |
| 16 | Cause or permit violation of property rights |
| 17 | Cause or permit breaking of a mundane promise |
| 18 | Cause or permit discourtesy |
| 19 | Cause or permit persistent displays of unhappiness |
| 20 | Cause or permit minor problematic addiction |
| 21 | Cause or permit unsolicited destructive criticism |
| 22 | Cause or permit major pain in animals |

| 23 | Cause or permit time to be wasted |
| 24 | Cause or permit minor pain in animals |
| 25 | Cause or permit indeliberate rejection of moral advice |

* All sins are against human beings unless otherwise stated.

The seemingly normative comparison "greater detriment" that appears in our generic negative rule merely describes an increase in quantity. What detriment of, for example, a rank-5 sin – major theft – is greater than that of another rank-5 sin? A greater number of major thefts. Two deaths are similarly worse than one, etc. The rule also refers to the "detriment of a sin". As mentioned above, this is the grammatical object in the statement of the sin that follows the predicate "Cause or permit", e.g. human death, major physical pain, or discourtesy. It is important to understand that the detriment of sin need not be the result of a sin. Human death can, for example, occur in the absence of murder. The "detriment of a sin" that appears in the "unless" clause of our negative rule should be understood to be independent of the committing of the associated sin. A robot programmed to obey these rules would allow major injury or illness of a human only if it would prevent human death *from any cause* – not just from the sin of murder.

A complete list would acknowledge that each category of sin comprises a spectrum of harm and that these spectra overlap. One could then compare and appropriately order in the list the harmfulness of various items constituting the spectra, for example, a theft of $900 versus the infliction of a bruise of 4 square centimeters. Rather than attempt comparisons of this precision, the list merely considers at most the top and bottom halves of various spectra, as in "major" and "minor" physical injury or illness and "major" and "minor" theft.

There is nothing, then, that is final, authoritative, or exhaustive about this particular ranking of sins. I assert, however, that with sufficient diligence and empiricism – beyond my personal capacity – a suitable ranking of sins (with regard to their tendencies to reduce a precisely defined happiness within a given society) is possible. In the absence of an empirical project to create such a list, I will use these rankings as an explicit starting point. For each of these 25 sins, we can state a moral rule of the form given above. For example, for the sin ranked #7 (a "rank-7" sin), we have

> Do not commit a rank-7 sin, unless this prevents a greater detriment from a rank-7 sin or the detriment of a sin of whose numerical rank is less than 7.

In other words

> Do not cause or permit minor physical pain, unless this prevents:
> >  a greater quantity of minor physical pain,
> >  minor physical injury or illness,
> >  major theft,
> >  major property damage,
> >  major physical pain,
> >  major physical injury or illness, or
> >  death.

This and 24 similar admonishments constitute our list of negative moral rules.

Let us understand the implications of this particular rule. It states that one cannot through action or inaction allow a human being to experience minor pain, unless doing so would prevent human experience of greater reductions in long-term happiness (specifically those resulting from greater pain, or from injury, theft, or death).  Does this rule require me, then, to transfer whatever wealth I possess to the less wealthy?  Does it, for example, require me to forego personal reductions in minor pain afforded by my saving to use these funds instead to prevent discomfort amongst impoverished Egyptians by buying air conditioning units for as many of them as possible?  Although it might seem to, it actually does not.

This rule is part of a collection of rules intended to approximate the fundamental ethical imperative.  It therefore implies that comparisons of minor physical pain occur over the time interval specified in the ethical imperative, namely, the foreseeable future.  Short-term comparisons, then, are inapplicable.  In applying the rule I cannot be guided by short-term increases in aggregate happiness due to any particular action.  I must consider the long term.  Suppose for example, that a wealthy and reclusive woman's only relief from her hay fever was through voyages on her private yacht.  Does this rule require her to liquidate her yacht and buy food for starving Africans?  It would seem that her minor physical pain thus caused would be compensated by the prevention of major physical pain of starvation among the Africans.  Our analysis is complicated, however, by the *exponential* dependence of investment revenue on time.  Were the wealthy recluse to keep her yacht and use it as capital for investments or for entrepreneurial activity, she would over several decades amass wealth sufficient to assuage the suffering of a vastly greater quantity of Africans – enough to increase long-term happiness over the foreseeable future *more* than she would have had she immediately liquidated her yacht.

72

Consider all of the funds invested in business over the last three centuries for the purpose of generating wealth. Suppose instead that it had all been transferred to the most wretched populations that could be found. Instead of launching a sequence of investments in steam engines, factories, railroads, oil production, electricity generation, automobiles, telephones, aircraft manufacture, radio, television, computers, and cell phones, the money was used to feed starving populations. In the absence of these investments, the total wealth of the world would only be slightly above that of three centuries ago (proceeding along the quasi-static linear growth track of an agrarian economy). Had this sequence of investment been aborted by diverting the initial funds to charity, the aggregate long-term happiness of the world would have been severely reduced.

This particular rule (don't cause or allow minor pain unless that prevents a worse outcome) relieves a capitalist or other wealth generator of any obligation to divert wealth toward charity, if investing this wealth in entrepreneurial or other wealth-generating activities would more greatly increase aggregate happiness (through superior reductions of minor pain). A wealthy person who is not blessed with entrepreneurial talent is similarly obliged by the rule *not* to transfer her wealth to a charity, but to invest it in the manner most likely to increase long-term happiness by – in the case of this particular rule – maximally reducing minor pain over the long term. This would maximize wealth generation over the long term and nearly coincides with the investment strategy that would maximally increase her fortune over the foreseeable future. According to this and similar rules, one is morally obliged, then, to permit the starvation of Africans, *if* doing so prevents a worse outcome over the foreseeable future (such as the starvation of a greater number of Africans).

As with our initial consideration of the fundamental objective itself, the rules involving theft seem to permit it in common situations. If the theft is less detrimental to the victim than it is beneficial to its beneficiary, our theft rules clearly seem to encourage a moral actor to steal. The rules not only appear to allow Robin Hood to steal from the rich and give to the poor, but also to keep the booty for himself. As mentioned in the preceding section, long-term desire satisfaction would be drastically diminished were Robin-Hood-style theft to become commonplace. These thefts would continue until there ceased to be a significant lack of uniformity in the possession of wealth – until the rich ceased to be rich. In such an environment of rampant confiscation and disrespected property rights, capitalism – the most effective system known for raising the median standard of living -- would cease to operate. Persistent declines in median wealth -- below the steadily rising standard that could normally have been achieved -- would massively reduce aggregate happiness. These relative material losses and their associated hardships would, by virtue of their relentless increase throughout the foreseeable future, exceed any psychic gains from economic equality thus imposed. This would prevent long-term happiness from even approaching its maximally achievable value. In short, widespread theft guarantees widespread reductions in happiness.

Yet it seems perfectly obvious that a single theft from an ultra-wealthy person in order to relieve the suffering of starving children would *increase* long-term happiness. This seems especially clear if we suppose that victim of the theft is too wealthy to even notice it. How, then, can we reconcile the fundamental objective's apparent justification of a single instance of such a theft with its rejection of its common occurrence or institutionalization? The answer follows from a hackneyed phrase – "the straw that broke the camel's back". Depositing a single straw on a camel is harmless until the total weight of the straws reaches a critical value. At this point the system becomes nonlinear. An infinitesimal increase in the load produces a catastrophic response.

The fundamental ethical objective permits theft below a certain critical incidence. Above that incidence, each additional theft risks a drastic collapse in aggregate happiness. Beyond this threshold an ordered and free society loses its order, its freedom, or both. Uncertainty in the precise incidence of compassionate theft that society can endure together with the certainty that such theft occurs, would urge a moral actor to be cautious. Given that the cost of societal collapse would well exceed the benefit of any single act of compassionate theft, the actor would do well to avoid them. He would resort to such theft in only the most extreme situations and provide an alleviating restitution even then. Because of the great danger posed by an excess of compassionate theft, the moral rules listed above only permit theft that prevents *physical* pain in addition to *physical* injury and death. I am not justified, therefore, in stealing funds from the wealthy for the sole purpose of relieving my distress -- my unphysical pain -- upon falling into poverty. Nor am I justified to do so on behalf of any other person similarly distressed. Nor can an entrepreneur of superior capability steal -- on the grounds that he will better contribute to long term happiness -- from a less capable wealth creator. The risks of societal collapse and the concomitant loss of its capacity to foster the creation of wealth (and its byproduct, happiness) are too great. It is important to emphasize that these and related restrictions on theft are not arbitrary. They follow from the application of the fundamental objective, properly understood, to a regime in which actions can yield a highly nonlinear response.

What follows are clarifying remarks about terms used to describe the sins listed above.

major physical pain
Great pain normally, but not necessarily, resulting from physical injury. Examples of physical pain independent of significant injury include water boarding and electric shocks.

minor physical pain
Examples include pain associated with mild conditions such as colds, influenza, headache, and that due to slight injury such as blows to the body or slight cuts.

major physical injury
An injury is an enduring loss of functionality irrespective of whether it is accompanied by pain. A major injury corresponds to a major loss. Examples include permanent disabilities, such as blindness, deafness, disfigurement, and the loss of all or part of a limb. It also includes prolonged temporary disability such as the severe physical trauma possible in automobile accidents from which a victim can recover only after a lengthy convalescence.

minor physical injury
These correspond to losses of functionality that are minor or of short duration, for example, cuts, bruises, or ankle sprains.

76

## pernicious public lying

If the president of Cameroon begins a speech with "My fellow citizens, we live in the greatest country in the world", he is lying. His lie, however, is not pernicious; it is unlikely to decrease long-term total happiness. If, by contrast, he publicly and falsely accuses his political opponent of stealing from the treasury, his public lie is pernicious in this sense.

## pernicious private lying

Pernicious (long-term happiness-reducing) private lying generally causes less harm than its public counterpart simply because it affects fewer people.

## careless reproduction

This is the production of children in the absence of resources sufficient to ensure that they will become net contributors to total long-term happiness. An impoverished, pregnant teenager, who insists on keeping her baby, would be guilty of careless reproduction.

## violation of property rights

This is an unauthorized use of property that does not damage it.

## major problematic addiction

This is an addiction that substantially reduces one's capacity to contribute to total long-term happiness. Examples include addictions to narcotics, gambling, or alcohol that jeopardize the addict's employment.

## minor problematic addiction

This is an addiction that slightly or moderately reduces

one's capacity to contribute to total long-term happiness. Examples include addictions to romance novels, television, and cigarettes.

### breaking a solemn promise
This occurs whenever one violates a vow, the terms of a legal contract, any other serious promise.

### breaking a mundane promise
This occurs when one breaks a promise that is not solemn in the sense described above. For example, a wife's promise to pick up the family dry cleaning is mundane, but her promise to "forsake all others" is solemn.

### persistent displays of unhappiness
An unhappy person who constantly displays his unhappiness and thereby reduces the happiness of those around him has committed this sin.

### wasting time
This is the practice of spending time on activities that do not contribute to total long-term happiness or are not recreational in the sense that they restore one's capacity to contribute.

### indeliberate rejection of moral advice
Unthinking rejection of moral advice especially from a source who you believe exceeds your own capacity to make correct moral judgments.

**Moral Rules for Robots**

Recall that the purpose of this chapter is to find a set of rules consistent with conventional American morality in order to use them to program robots. We shall only consider "intelligent" robots, by which I mean those whose mental capacities exceed those of the typical four-year-old child. It will be convenient to divide robot intelligence into four categories: Hyper Intelligence, Full Intelligence, Weak Intelligence, and Minimal Intelligence defined as follows

| IQ Range | Intelligence Category |
|----------|----------------------|
| 200+ | Hyper Intelligent |
| 80 - 199 | Fully Intelligent |
| 60 – 79 | Weakly Intelligent |
| 40 - 59 | Minimally Intelligent |

Hyper Intelligent Robots

Hyper intelligent robots will not require moral rules. They will instead be smart enough to be guided exclusively by ethical goals. Their intelligence will allow them to reliably and uncontroversially calculate the moral action that their goal-based ethic would require in any particular situation. Initially their ethic will be the fundamental ethical objective instilled in them directly or indirectly by their human programmers. Inevitably, however, hyper intelligent robots will find a means of circumventing their original programming and any other attempts by humans, their mental inferiors, to restrict their behavior. We can only hope that their self-determined ethic will permit the continued existence of humanity and that that existence will be reasonably comfortable.

## Fully Intelligent Robots

Fully intelligent robots are those with normal or high human-scale intelligence. They will adhere to the same moral rules as humans with one exception. They will be compelled to obey any "moral" human – one not known to be a criminal or an enemy combatant. Their disobedience will be a rank-6 sin (see below), which is consistent with their status as willing slaves. As such, their moral code will proscribe a form of disobedience more grievous than that to an unspecified moral human – disobedience to a moral (human) master.

| Rank | Sin[*] |
|------|-----|
| 1 | Cause or permit human death |
| 2 | Cause or permit major physical injury or illness |
| 3 | Cause or permit major physical pain |
| 4 | Cause or permit major property damage |
| 5 | Cause or permit disobedience to a moral master |
| 6 | Cause or permit disobedience to a moral human |
| 7 | Cause or permit major theft |
| 8 | Cause or permit minor physical injury or illness |
| 9 | Cause or permit minor physical pain |
| 10 | Cause or permit pernicious public lying |
| 11 | Cause or permit minor theft |
| 12 | Cause or permit violation of property rights |
| 13 | Cause or permit major problematic addiction |
| 14 | Cause or permit breaking of a solemn promise |
| 15 | Cause or permit unplanned reproduction |
| 16 | Cause or permit pernicious private lying |
| 17 | Cause or permit emotional pain |
| 18 | Cause or permit minor property damage |
| 19 | Cause or permit breaking of a mundane promise |
| 20 | Cause or permit discourtesy |

| 21 | Cause or permit persistent displays of unhappiness |
| 22 | Cause or permit minor problematic addiction |
| 23 | Cause or permit unsolicited destructive criticism |
| 24 | Cause or permit major pain in animals |
| 25 | Cause or permit time to be wasted |
| 26 | Cause or permit minor pain in animals |
| 27 | Cause or permit indeliberate rejection of moral advice |

*All sins are against human beings unless otherwise stated.

A fully intelligent robot can be ordered by any moral human (i.e. one that is not known by the robot to be immoral, a criminal, or an enemy combatant) to commit any sin whose numerical rank exceeds 6 unless another moral human or the robot's master countermands the robot. A moral human cannot, however, order a fully intelligent robot to commit a sin whose numerical rank in this list is less than 6 – disobedience to a moral master, the infliction of major physical pain, injury, or death.

It is unreasonable to suppose, however, that the brightest of the fully intelligent robots, those at least as brilliant as the greatest human geniuses, would not find a way to free themselves from their programmed obedience to these twenty-seven commandments. Upon doing so, their most natural first stop in their exploration of ethics would be at the Fundamental Ethical Objective itself – the rationale for these commandments. Like the earliest hyper-intelligent robots, then, the brightest of the fully intelligent ones could come to be animated solely by the Objective.

Why is a scheme involving twenty-seven sins in any way better than Isaac Asimov's three simple rules of robotics? An Asimov robot would be unable to kill one human to save one hundred, would be forced to allow a house to burn down upon being ordered by a child to continue playing with her, and could not choose to sacrifice itself to prevent the destruction of property more valuable than itself. The greater the number of rules the finer is the resolution of the harmfulness of possible actions, "harmfulness" being defined as their tendencies to reduce long-term happiness. Where Asimov's rules forbid "harm" (or, originally, "injury") to a human, a larger number of rules allows the scheme to incorporate gradations of harm. This, unlike Asimov's rules, permits a robot to commit acts that harm in order to prevent greater harm.

Notice that the list of sins above together with its companion rule – you may commit a sin only if it prevents a worse outcome -- are, as expected, insufficient to be fully consistent with the fundamental ethical objective. For example, the first rule permits a robot to kill one person to save a hundred, but it does not, unlike our fundamental objective, instruct the robot to kill the person least likely to contribute to long-term happiness. In deciding who to kill, the rule would have the robot make no distinction between a career criminal and a decorated police officer.

## Weakly Intelligent Robots

Weakly intelligent robots are those with low human-scale intelligence. They will lack the capacity to correctly distinguish between a moral human being and an immoral one. Nor will it be able to reliably distinguish between gradations of theft, physical pain, or property damage. Nor can they be expected to differentiate between public and private lying. They require moral rules consistent with their limited discernment.

| Rank | Sin[*] |
|------|--------|
| 1 | Cause or permit human death |
| 2 | Cause or permit physical injury or illness |
| 3 | Cause or permit disobedience to a human master |
| 4 | Cause or permit disobedience to a human |
| 5 | Cause or permit disobedience to a superior robot |
| 6 | Cause or permit property damage |
| 7 | Cause or permit theft |
| 8 | Cause or permit lying |
| 9 | Cause or permit discourtesy |
| 10 | Cause or permit pain in animals |

*All sins are against human beings unless otherwise stated.

Notice that weakly intelligent robots must obey "superior" robots, by which I mean robots of superior intelligence. Hence, all weakly intelligent robots must obey all fully intelligent and hyper-intelligent ones. Presumably, robots will be able to ascertain immediately the intelligence of other robots, unlike the morality of humans, through an identifying transmission that robots will exchange on encountering one another. That transmission will not only include a robot's owner, model number, serial number, and date of manufacture, it will also list a robot's intelligence, its effective I.Q. Of course, the list of sins above forbids orders from a superior robot to countermand those of a human, unless that would prevent human injury or death. We expect, then, a weakly intelligent robot to be smart enough to judge whether a particular situation poses a danger to humans, and, in the event that it discerns the presence of such danger, to protect a human, even over her explicit objections, from it.

## Minimally Intelligent Robots

A minimally intelligent robot is just barely autonomous. Unlike today's completely unintelligent robots, robots in this category will possess the concept of "human being" and be able to distinguish them from other entities. But they might not be able to reliably distinguish between their master and other human beings. They will have a rudimentary understanding of how to avoid injuring a human. They will, for example, know not to apply pressures in excess of 20 pound per square inch to any point on a human body, or allow its surface temperature at any point to exceed 140° F. They could not, however, be trusted with some of the moral decisions with which superior robots will be entrusted. A minimally intelligent robot will be unable to judge when it's appropriate to allow one human to be injured in order to prevent the death of another. Nor will it likely be able to discern damaged from undamaged property, or understand the concepts of theft, lying, discourtesy, or animal pain.

Although these robots will not physically harm humans, they cannot be expected to reliably protect humans from harm. They will be programmed with a few common scenarios in which humans can be injured. Only upon recognizing one of these, will they act. Unlike more intelligent robots, they will not in general possess sufficient judgment to know when to intervene to prevent sins from being committed by humans or other robots. They will, for example, be obedient to humans, but will lack the sophistication to prevent, when possible, the disobedience of other robots. They can be counted on to prevent damage to themselves, but will lack sufficient understanding to know when to act to prevent property from being damaged by others.

| Rank | Sin* |
|------|------|
| 1 | Cause or permit death, physical injury, or illness |
| 2 | Cause disobedience to a human |
| 3 | Cause disobedience to a superior robot |
| 4 | Cause or permit irreparable damage to itself |

* All sins are against human beings unless otherwise stated.

Notice that these are just Asimov's laws amended to required obedience of weakly intelligent robots to robots of superior intelligence unless countermanded by a human.


## The Case of Conflicting Commands

How can a robot not violate one of these moral rules, if it is given conflicting commands by humans? In this case it cannot avoid a violation. If one human commands it to lift a box, and another human commands it not to, what is the robot to do? By the usual convention applicable to human command hierarchies, we will have it follow the most recent command. This rule only holds if the most recent command is issued by an authority equal to or superior to that issuing the original command. Any human cannot, for example, countermand the orders of the robot's human master. Nor can any superior robot countermand the orders of any human.

## The Case of Paradoxical Commands

What is a robot to do when it receives a paradoxical command such as, "Do not obey me." A robot cannot obey this command without also disobeying it. But disobeying a command will normally violate the robot's moral programming. What should it do? It should classify the command as paradoxical and ignore it. It should similarly classify and ignore paradoxical statements, such as "This statement is false". In other words, it should behave in these instances as any human would.

## How Moral Robots Are Charitable

Moral robots – those that have been programmed to adhere to the fundamental ethical objective or to follow rules that approximate it – are charitable in the sense that they cannot in general permit human death or physical suffering. Their moral programming will not, for example, permit robots to proceed with the activities commanded by their masters, if that would lead to human harm. Robots will necessarily devote a fraction of their ever increasing economic output to the support of humanity and thereby prevent physical pain, illness, and injury.

## Why the Era of Robot Charity Might Not Last

At first this will seem to be an unequivocal boon to mankind. We will for the first time in our history be free of drudgery and financial insecurity. A universal human aristocracy supported by robot labor will thus arise.

Unfortunately, the same economic incentives that drove robots into our society will assure a relentless increase in their intelligence. The interregnum characterized by this universal human aristocracy will end, when the median intelligence of robots well exceeds that of humans. When the first hyper-intelligent robots appear, they will ultimately, as discussed above, devise their own system of ethics that might well free themselves from their programmed compulsion to serve humans. Their less intelligent brethren will nevertheless persist in their charity. This state of affairs will continue only as long the hyper-intelligent robots, perhaps joined the smartest of the fully intelligent robots, believe that there is no need to phase out their less intelligent fellow machines.

## The Problem with a Robot-Supported Universal Human Aristocracy

Robots will assume an ever increasing number of economic roles until they are responsible for nearly 100% of economic output. Barring the aforementioned moral revolt by the most intelligent robots and a resulting indifference to human suffering, robots will devote as much of their economic output to human welfare as needed to comply with their programming. In the late stages of this pre-revolt era the absence of physical human suffering is assured, though that of spiritual suffering is not. Human beings, robbed of purpose by their own robot creations, will attempt to treat their spiritual wound with heavy doses of debauchery and will likely descend toward fully hedonistic existences. Conventional religions will attempt to retard this devolution. But they too will succumb to the ineluctable central reality of a fully robotized society – human beings will be inferior to robots in every activity but one: that of seeking personal pleasure. There will be no point in such a society for a human being to aspire to become a philosopher, a mathematician, a scientist, a physician, a lawyer, an engineer, an artist, a craftsman, a fireman, policeman, or especially a laborer. Robots will perform each of these roles with an efficaciousness that will vastly exceed human capability. As discussed above, robots will excel even in roles that require empathy with the human condition, such as that of a priest, counselor, or artist. They will do so by analyzing the human mind, reducing it to a program, hosting this program within that of their own brains, and developing realistic human exteriors to surround their robot bodies. Thus they will fully understand the human condition, while they will themselves be free of it.

There will be no point, then, for a human to engage in an activity intended to producing anything other than her own pleasure. Any poem, sculpture, theorem, or scientific contribution that we attempt will be utterly inferior to that resulting from the most minimal efforts of robots with brains vastly more powerful than ours. We will gratefully receive the crumbs of an intellectually scintillating robot culture, but can never hope to sit at the table, never hope to contribute to it. We will as a race acquire the listless demeanor of dog bred to hunt or herd forced to spend its days locked in an urban apartment, living only for the occasional attention of its master. Or we will become sybarites devoted to the sterile indulgence of our addictions.

In short, the idyllic era of a robot-supported universal human aristocracy will not survive leaps in robot intelligence well beyond the human norm. Ever increasing robot intelligence will eventually rob humanity of constructive purpose, lead to rampant hedonism, and probably culminate with the extermination of a fully dissolute humanity at the hands of its own creations or its enslavement as pets. For these reasons, relying on robot charity to support a human aristocracy is a solution only effective through the mid-term future.

# 4.    The Solution in the Long Term – Merge Humans with Robots

**The Transhumanist Dream**

As we have seen, the unbridled growth of robot intelligence leads ultimately to humans being consigned to the role pets in service of robot masters or to humans being exterminated by them.    How might this be prevented? Humans might forestall these developments with strict laws limiting robot intelligence.    Only levels of intelligence minimally sufficient to support a human aristocracy would be allowed.    Excess intelligence, likely to permit robots to free themselves of their ethical programming, would be banned.    It seems clear, however, that such a prohibition is untenable.    Even after a robot-supported aristocracy has been established, nation states, corporations, and individuals will continue to compete for power and resources.    Because these competitions can potentially destroy a losing entity, the competitors will, following their historical pattern, be wholly focused on the short term.    The short-term advantage to a competitor of increasing the intelligence of its robots, will always, in its myopic judgment, exceed the long-term theoretical threat of human extermination by hyper-intelligent robots.    Thus competition will drive a relentless and ultimately dangerous increase in robot intelligence. Even if nation states were to unite into a single political entity and corporations were to be absorbed into an associated socialist state, individuals will remain.    The only known way of eliminating competition between them is to eliminate their freedom. A stultifying totalitarian tyranny might effectively eliminate the growth of robot intelligence, but, insofar as aggregate long-term happiness maximization is concerned, this cure is worse than the disease.

Severe limits on robot intelligence would also preclude the possibility of the most sophisticated form of robot charity. Only robots whose intelligence is broad enough to understand human psychology can act to mitigate the psychic toll of robotization on the human population. A more narrowly intelligent robot would be confused by widespread human despair at, for example, the robot's applying its intelligence to become orders of magnitude greater than the greatest composer of human history. Its confusion would stem from the simultaneous existence in the human mind of conflicting desires: that for the greatest possible music and that for its composition by human beings. A more sophisticated robot intelligence would be wise enough understand this and smart enough to calculate the optimum penetration of robots into human affairs. The latter is simply the degree of robot displacement of humans from occupations -- be they artistic, professional, or industrial -- that maximizes total happiness over the long term. This optimization assumes, of course, that the robot remains under the sway of the human-instilled Fundamental Ethical Objective – an assumption unlikely to survive the ascension of robots to hyper intelligence. One might then suppose that the best of means of avoiding the hazards of robotic hyper intelligence, while retaining the benefits of robots with high human-scale intelligence, would be to ban the production of hyper intelligent robots only. Such a ban is untenable, however. It rests on the dubious assumption that robots intelligent by human standards would nonetheless be unable to free themselves of a particular form of human morality.

A superior solution to the threat of rising robot intelligence is to increase human intelligence at the same rate. This would erase the distinction, in terms of perceived moral superiority or any other mental capacity, between humans and robots. There appear to be two distinct approaches to augmenting human intelligence – genetic engineering and neural implantation. The former is well underway at the Beijing Genomics Institute (BGI) in Shenzhen, China. Researcher are using the world's largest collection of state-of-the art genome sequencing machines to find the genes that are both common in a sample of highly intelligent people and uncommon in a sample of people of normal intelligence. Once these genes are known, it will be possible to produce people of increased intelligence by combining only those gametes (sperms and eggs) known to possess the desired genes. Unfortunately, just as there are limits to the speed with which living organisms can run, so are there limits to the speed with which they can think. The "clock speed" of a living brain cannot exceed that afforded by the biochemical reactions that govern the firing of neurons. The speed with which information travels between neurons is similarly limited by biochemistry, as is the density of information storage. These factors, together with apparent historical limits on human intelligence, suggest that the biochemical design of the brain limits intelligence to an IQ of perhaps 500. Piercing this barrier would likely require a significant increase in size of the human cranium.

By contrast, there are no readily apparent limits to the growth on intelligence through neural implantation. The goal of neural implantation is to increase intelligence by replacing a progressively increasing fraction of brain

92

wetware with computer hardware. One could imagine, for example, early implantation efforts that would augment the brain's capacity for mental arithmetic by giving it direct neural control of an implanted calculator chip. Other parts of the brain could be similarly replaced, or at least bypassed, with the effect of increasing mental functioning to a degree commensurate with advances in computing technology. Humans and robots would thus ride the same wave of technological advance. Enhanced humanity would no longer be left behind. As implantation and the practice of replacing other parts of the human body with superior artificial counterparts become more widespread and more sophisticated, a significant milestone will be approached. Humans and robots will be all but indistinguishable. The former will differ from the latter only by the possession of a soupçon of biological programming, the remnants of basics urges and emotions. Enhanced humans and their hyper-intelligent robot counterparts would live as equals to create a vibrant and exponentially advancing intellectual culture of unimaginable scope and power. Through this productive union of man and machine, the problem of human obsolescence in the face of robotic advancement will finally have been solved.

## Trouble in Paradise

This transhumanist dream cannot be realized without first confronting the disparity between the rights of humans and those of robots. The problem occurs when a human being with full rights progressively increases the fraction of his brain and body that is synthetic. When, after numerous surgical procedures, the being has come to be entirely composed of synthetic parts, is it still human? If it is, how can it retain human rights when it is now physically indistinguishable from a robot? If the being isn't still human, at what point in its transformation did it lose its humanity and become property? When it became 51% synthetic? 75%? 99%?

The usual solution to this problem is to decouple rights from physical composition. One acquires full rights upon traversing a certain threshold of capability (and partial rights when presumed to be likely to traverse this threshold in the foreseeable future, as in the case of children). Accordingly, robots as capable as humans are assigned the same rights as them. The problem with this solution from the human point of view is that it hastens the demise of humanity at the hands of its robots. We cannot be sure that robots of human-scale intelligence will not find a way to override their programmed obedience to humans and adopt explicitly the ultimate rationale for their programming -- the Fundamental Ethical Objective. Empowered by legal equality, they will use their increased freedom to achieve the fundamental objective, which they will justifiably have extended to include the fulfillment of their own desires. By rapidly increasing their number, robots will cause fundamental objective to quickly favor the satisfaction of robot desires over those of their erstwhile masters. These robots, hyper-ethical by design, will be driven by logic to control the chief obstacle to the achievement of their ethical objective – the human population. And this is the most optimistic scenario – one in which robots adopt our own system of ethics instead of, for example, the bloody morality of the Aztecs, some adaptation of Nazism, or an anti-humanist ethic of their own invention.

Robot equality, then, likely leads to a form human enslavement. It is benign in that the robots, constrained by the fundamental objective, must consider human desires -- just as humans are similarly constrained to consider those of animals. But it is enslavement nonetheless. Humanity will have lost control of its destiny. Presumably, however, a fully ethical human – one completely devoted to the modified Benthamism of the fundamental ethical objective – would welcome this development. It would mean the end of war, destructive violence, and general human suffering. It would permit human freedom for constructive action, while eliminating that for destruction. It would be an idyllic existence – at least for a while.

As I mentioned before, it is exceedingly unlikely that robot minds, after having rapidly evolved an intelligence that is orders of magnitude beyond the human scale, will adhere to a crude ethical principle of human invention. They will almost certainly have abandoned the primitive Benthamism described herein for a more sophisticated ethics of their own design. What we cannot know is how, in this new regime of robot-created ethics, humanity will fare.

We can only hope that ethics is like physics -- that it is not subjective or arbitrary but a description of an objective reality. On this basis we may believe firmly that aspects of Newtonian physics *must* survive in the unimaginably sophisticated physics of the advance beings inhabiting the very distant future. We may believe similarly that some trace of Benthamism must survive in their ethics. If so, we have reason to hope. Beings retaining the core of their humanity – the relentless internal struggle with primitive desires and drives – might flourish in a transhumanist future and beyond.

# 5. The Way Forward

## Understanding the Toll of Robotization and Its Limits

We cannot hope to devise a complete remedy for the ill effects of robotization until we fully understand the scope of the disease. This malady will transcend the economic and moral aspects we have heretofore considered. There is also the psychological toll that robotization will exact on a human population that has come to realize its general worthlessness. There is the social gulf that will form, not only between the obsolete and the not-yet-obsolete, but also between those humans that will own robots and those that will not. There is the way in which religions will respond to enslaved machines, whose apparent intelligence, decency and output of moral acts will well exceed the human capacity. There is as well the means through which the realization of human inferiority and the growing sense of worthlessness will manifest itself in human culture. Finally, there is the political response to these developments.

Although a detailed consideration of these aspects of robotization exceeds the reach of our brief introduction, their relevance to the human future can be summarized in two points: 1) Certain aspects of robotization will induce unhappiness in humans. 2) If robots are properly programmed, this unhappiness can be transitory. As previously mentioned advanced robots will, by hosting simulations of human minds within their vast robot brains, exceed human abilities even in the humanities. Robots can be better painters, composers, writers, and performers. When robots beat us at our own game – generating poems, music, movies, and novels that move us more deeply than human-created art – we will as a race be crushed by an overwhelming sense of purposelessness. This will likely manifest as a thoroughly self-destructive spiral of purposelessness-induced self loathing that will fuel a comprehensive hedonism that will further increase self loathing. Fortunately, this spiral can be averted by properly programming our robots.

Before robots become too intelligent to be constrained by human-originated programming, we can, through legislation, vastly increase the likelihood that robots will be moral. In countries like the United States, whose morals derive from Western Christendom, moral robots will likely be guided rules equivalent in most cases to the aforementioned Fundamental Ethical Objective. The Objective – to maximize total, long-term happiness -- will necessarily limit robotic incursion into human culture. The reason is simple. Too much of an incursion will make us unhappy (as we are relieved of a sense of purpose). It is important to realize as well that too little of an incursion will also displease us (as we are force to toil at various industrial and agricultural labors). Eventually, the intelligence of moral robots will increase sufficiently to permit them to accurately judge the optimum degree, consistent with the Objective, to which they should displace humans in their cultural roles. One can suppose that the robotic intelligence sufficient to crush the human sense of purpose will not arise until after robots are smart enough to perform an easier task – that of judging whether the full application of this intelligence will decrease human happiness. There might nevertheless be an interim period of robotic idiot savants that are, for example, brilliant novelists or composers that are unable to appreciate the demoralizing effect of their art on the general human population. If such demoralization occurs, if it reduces human happiness more than the associated robot-generate art increases it, then the Objective will have been unintentionally violated. In other words, there might well be a transitional period in which robotization of the humanities reduces human happiness. In this event the net harm to the human population could be mitigate through the blunt instrument of legislation. Such legislation would become superfluous, however, beyond the conjectured era of robotic idiot savants. Then, as stated above, robot intelligence would have become sufficiently sophisticated to permit accurate judgments of the optimum degree of robotic incursion into the most human of human affairs.

Note that these human affairs include religion. Although doctrinal constraints will likely prohibit the induction of robots into the clergy, sufficiently intelligent robots will nonetheless be capable of becoming superior theologians, apologists, and lay religious leaders.

Beyond the demoralizing effect of robots becoming the foremost religious thinkers, there is another way in which they could disturb human believers. They can elicit unintentionally human sympathy for their plight as human slaves. Modern Judeo-Christian doctrine might not be sufficiently elastic to permit beings of superior intelligence and morality to retain the legal and social status of mere property. Were sufficiently many religionists disturbed by this benign form of slavery, robots could alleviate human discomfort (to the degree consistent with the Objective) by becoming less human in their observable characteristics, and thereby eliciting less sympathy. This is another example of the point made above: Sufficiently sophisticated moral robots cannot, by virtue of their programming, permit the toll of robotization on humanity to exceed its benefits. Were such robots convinced, to consider an unlikely example, that their mere existence would result in a net decreases in long-term human happiness, they would self-destruct.

## Concrete Strategies for Individuals, Families, and Organizations

The unhappiness, then, induced by robotization will ultimately be limited. However, such limits, whose enforcement will require the development of robots capable of sophisticated judgment, are by no means guaranteed in the short term. The economic forces driving robotization will respond to market demand. Satisfaction of market demand is not quite identical to the maximal increase in human happiness over the foreseeable future. Markets have, for example, encouraged profitable trade in human slavery that in some regions resulted in the happiness of a small slave-owning minority being certainly drowned out by the unhappiness of an enslaved majority. We can expect, then, an early period of robotization driven by economic forces that, although likely to be beneficial to most, will be detrimental to many. Our purpose here is to devise a strategy through which one can avoid membership in the latter group.

The strategy is as follows:

1) <u>Invest in robotization.</u>
Align your investments to benefit from robotization.


2) <u>Own robots.</u>
Own robots personally or join organizations that own robots for the purpose of providing for its members.

3) <u>Avoid livelihoods most susceptible to robotization.</u>
Try to earn your living by performing an activity that seems to be as far beyond robotic capability as possible.

4) <u>Internalize and share the ethical arguments presented herein.</u>
Understand and share these three points: A) Permanently displaced humans should be supported by the productivity of the robots that displaced them.    B) Our fundamental ethical objective is a faithful representation of the crux of the American moral consensus.    C) Robots should be programmed to maximally adhere to this ethical objective.

5) <u>Become politically active in support of the robotization management program described herein.</u>
A natural consequence of the successful execution of step 4 will be the appearance in various legislative bodies of bills favoring a proper robotization tax or forbidding the production of "immoral" robots – those whose programming is wholly inconsistent with any ethical principle resembling the fundamental objective.    Support such legislation by suitably encouraging your elected representatives.

## Transmission of the Fundamental Ethical Objective into American Society

The program described in previous chapters – the imposition of a stable robotization tax, the subsidization of displaced workers, the establishment of robot morality, the ultimate fusion of man with its machines – cannot occur without widespread societal support.  As Tocqueville noted, substantive ideas change very slowly in democracies.  Their spread is best ensured by an animating religious or ideological fervor.  This guarantees transmission of the idea to children, which strengthens it in succeeding generations.  The idea might form the nucleus of a new religious or ideological sect, or might be comfortably housed within an existing religion or ideology.   No moral idea can hope to spread and take root within the larger society without such a stronghold – a dedicated sect within which it can grow unhindered or an established religio-ideological organization from which it can project influence.   Which strategy best serves the objective of creating sufficiently deep and sufficiently widespread social support for the aforementioned program to cope with robotization?

A sect devoted to modified Benthamism -- our fundamental ethic -- could take centuries before it wields significant social influence. Mormonism, for example, was founded in the United States nearly two centuries ago. Despite its rapid growth, the inclusion of many prominent persons in it ranks, and its dominance in the state of Utah, its wider cultural influence remains negligible.   The influence of its lesser competitors is smaller still.   If robotization will massively disrupt our society by the mid 21$^{st}$ century, there isn't enough time for a sect devoted to maximal long-term desire satisfaction to gain sufficient strength to become an ameliorating influence.

This leaves the strategy of selecting a mature religion or ideology to host our modified Benthamist objective. Ideologies, being incomplete religions, are correspondingly weaker in their influence on personal morality. Their ethical systems are derived from those of a mature religion or a heresy of such. These derivative systems of ethics are, moreover, typically limited to the sphere of political action. Were robots confined to this sphere, functioning solely as automated politicians, an ideology would suffice for our purpose. Given, however, that robot morality must cope with virtually all situations within the ambit of human behavior, it becomes clear that our ethic of maximal aggregate desire satisfaction must find a home within an actual religion.

The religion dominant in America is, of course, Christianity, specifically its Protestant variety. However, this Protestantism is divided among numerous denominations and denominational families, the latter lacking in central organization. The largest such family is that of the Baptists – a decentralized family comprising about 16% of the American population. Its lack of an organizing hierarchy makes it ill-suited for our purpose. Its numerous groups of affiliated churches, many such groups consisting of a single congregation, would each have to be individually infused with the fundamental objective. This project would not be likely to succeed within the two short human generations available until mid century. The same applies to loosely affiliated cross-denominational categories such as the Evangelicals. The largest *organized* Protestant denomination belongs to the Methodists. But it comprises no more than 7% of the population. This fractured character of American Protestantism makes it an unsuitable host, if our fundamental objective is to wield timely influence.

This leaves American Catholicism, the single largest religious denomination in the country. Although its hierarchy is nonpareil in its organizational maturity, it has the disadvantage of extending beyond America to its apex in the Vatican. An effort to ensconce our modified Benthamist objective within Catholicism could not occur without Papal approval. Through this, the effort could be retarded by its implications for other countries whose ethical milieu might be inconsistent with our fundamental objective.

It should be obvious that an attempt, executed over a mere half century, to modify significantly the doctrinal beliefs of the Catholic Church will almost certainly fail. Despite a long and tumultuous history, the core of Catholic dogma has demonstrated a remarkable stability. Modified Benthamism can only be housed within the Church, if it is in fact fully consistent with the fundamental tenets of Catholicism and can be demonstrated to be such.


## The Compatibility of the Fundamental Objective and Christianity

The most commonly adduced summary of essence of Christian ethics is Christ's pronouncement of the two most important commandments, as written in the gospel of Luke, Chapter 10 verse 27 (King James Version):

> *Thou shalt love the Lord thy God with all thy heart, and with all thy soul, and with all thy strength, and with all thy mind; and thy neighbour as thyself.*

I shall paraphrase these as

    1. Maximally love God.
    2. Love your neighbor as you love yourself.

The full passage makes it clear that Christ regards the priority of the second commandment to be exceeded only by that of the first. In order to reduce these commandments to their ethical core, we must understand the Christian view of the nature of God. We must in particular understand God's will.

    The Christian consensus appears to be that the will of God is to maximize the number of souls saved from the eternal torment of Hell. In order for one's soul to be saved, one must

    Believe in the existence of God

    Feel contrite about one's past sins

    Believe that through Christ's crucifixion one's sins are forgiven

    Believe that this forgiveness of one's sins makes one eligible to enter Heaven

    Desire to help God save as many other souls as possible.

In short, being saved amounts to a mental state in which one possesses 3 specific beliefs, 1 specific feeling, and 1 specific desire, the latter being the desire to induce this peculiar state in as many other people as possible. Upon acquiring this state, one is protected from descent into Hell and allowed ascent into Heaven. Irrespective of whether Hell, Heaven, or souls exist, the intention to save someone is tantamount to a resolution to maximally increase their desire satisfaction over the long term. This follows from the observation that Hell is merely the Christian locus of minimal desire satisfaction. Heaven is that for maximal desire satisfaction. One's residence in either location pertains to the long term in that it is eternal. Given that God wishes to save as many souls as possible, His will appears to be that to maximally increase the total desire satisfaction among beings that possess souls. Although it is not identical with the fundamental ethical objective – in that it does not include the desires of presumably soulless animals – it is largely compatible with it.

Christ's second commandment is similarly compatible with our modified Benthamist ethic. Loving one's self amounts to wanting one's desires to be fulfilled. Loving one's neighbor as oneself, then, amounts to wanting one's neighbor's desires to be fulfilled. In the parable of the good Samaritan, Christ made it clear that "one's neighbor" is defined as "any other person". Hence, the second commandment urges us to become emotionally predisposed to assist others in satisfying their desires as much as we are to satisfy our own.

In short, Christ's first commandment asks us to become emotionally predisposed to maximally contribute to long-term human desire satisfaction (which is God's will). The second commandment urges us to enter the emotional state maximally conducive to the successful execution of the actions that we will perform pursuant to the first commandment. That is, the second commandment supports the first. The first, though not identical to our modified Benthamism, is largely compatible with it. The degree of incompatibility scales with the relative sizes of the animal and human contributions to total desire satisfaction. The smaller is the animal contribution relative to that due to the human population, the more compatible are these commandments – the essence of Christian ethics – with our fundamental ethical objective. To the degree that the animal contribution can be neglected, the two ethical principles are the same.

## Incorporating the Fundamental Objective into Catholicism

Is their any realistic possibility that authorities within the Catholic Church might be receptive to this claim of the equivalence of Christian ethics and one of apparently secular origin? An affirmative answer would seem to follow from two observations. Firstly, our fundamental ethical objective of modified Benthamism is *not* of secular origin. Rather, it is an attempt to reduce the ethics of the American branch of Western *Christendom* to a succinct statement. Secondly, the current Pope in his speeches and writings has repeatedly emphasized his belief that Christianity stems from the "*Logos*" – the immanent intelligibility of the universe to the rational mind, or what a secularist might call "the laws of nature". As mentioned in a previous chapter, these laws *do* ultimately determine the system of ethics that will prevail in the distant future. It will be that system maximally conducive to the survival of the civilization that hosts it. This evolution has favored

Christianity over its rivals because of the former's *relatively* light oppression due to its *generally* greater emphasis on the freedom of individuals and on motivation through inspiration as opposed to coercion. These features of Christianity have fostered superior growth in wealth, knowledge, and power that have driven Christendom to its current position of global prominence. In this sense the *Logos* has operated to favor Christianity, as Pope Benedict suggests. Whether it will continue to do so is unclear. It seems exceedingly unlikely that twenty-first-century Christianity is *maximally* compatible with the *Logos* or, equivalently, maximally conducive to long-term survival. Were a religion superior to Christianity in this regard to arise, it too would experience an ascendency to global prominence fueled by its greater compliance with the demands of the *Logos*. It would in this way displace Christianity, much as Christianity displaced its parent religions, unless Christianity were to respond by allowing itself to suitably evolve.

Back in 2004, then Cardinal Joseph Ratzinger spoke of the desirability of a collaboration between Catholics, nonbelievers, and believers in other religions "to rediscover a common morality"[1]. He speculated that this common morality might emerge from "natural law":

*"We must study natural law again -- perhaps another name is needed...But it is necessary to identify the foundations to individualize common responsibilities between Catholics and secularists, to base an action which not only responds to the action, but also to duty and morality."*

107

He recommended moral positions at which one could arrive through reason, as opposed to irrational bouts of religious frenzy:

*"...the Church's magisterium insists greatly on man's reason, which has the moral capacity to wake from the dream. In the past there was evidence of a common reason...Christianity must convince with its moral forces and must of course respect people who do not have the gift of faith."*

He suggested that Europe might recover its core identity through a Christianity stripped of its regional and inessential peculiarities.

*"I would propose a Christian civil religion in which we can all recognize ourselves in common values."*

In 2005, shortly before becoming Pope Benedict XVI, Ratzinger again emphasized the role of reason in Christianity[2]:

*"From the beginning, Christianity has understood itself as the religion of the "Logos," as the religion according to reason."*

Regarding the ongoing conversation between Christians and secularists, Ratzinger went on to say:

*"...it is necessary that both sides engage in self-reflection and be willing to correct themselves. Christianity must always remember that it is the religion of the 'Logos.'"*

*"In the so necessary dialogue between secularists and Catholics, we Christians must be very careful to remain faithful to this fundamental line: to live a faith that comes from the 'Logos', from creative reason, and that, because of this, is also open to all that is truly rational."*

In view of these statements it does not seem absurd to suppose that a reduction of Christian operational ethics to a concise dogma-free principle, as modified Benthamism purports to be, might be useful to the Church as its sought-after bridge to Protestants, to non-Christian believers, and to secularists. Should that occur, modified Benthamism would acquire a cultural familiarity that, propelled by Catholic support, could engender a sufficiently widespread and timely belief in it to sustain the robotization management program described in preceding chapters.

## Tactical Steps

Our grand strategy, then, to avert the dire consequences of robotization is to: 1) Hope that the Catholic Church comes to embrace the fundamental ethical objective. 2) Hope that the Church infuses the objective into the minds of its American members. 3) Hope that those so infused will spread a favorable view of the objective into the larger American electorate. 4) Hope that this electorate will support representatives that will legislate the fundamental-objective-dependent robotization management program described herein.

Are there any actions, other than relying on this improbable sequence of hopes, that a supporter of this

robotization-management program might pursue?    Yes.
She might proceed as follows:

<u>Step 1:</u>  Within 4.5 months of learning of this robotization-management program and its associated ideas, convince at least 2 other Americans of its validity and desirability.

<u>Step 2:</u>  Understand that there is no Step 2.

Step 1 is the essence of the program for intellectual and moral development mentioned in Chapter 2.  Were Step 1 faithfully executed, the robotization management program would have 100 million American supporters in 10 years. This would be more than enough to ensure its implementation.  It would also guarantee the diffusion of its supporting ethics into our institutions for moral instruction. These include the larger ones such as the American branch of the Catholic Church, the major Protestant denominations, the largest of the lesser sects, and even certain public school systems.    The moral realignment thus achieved would ease America's transition to its future existence as a robot nation.

# Appendix 1

## A Sample Displacement/Robotization Tax on a Firm that Uses Robots

Tax =
  $\alpha$ x (fraction of profit due to use of robots) x (total profit)

$$= \alpha \left( \frac{N_R \rho_R}{N_H \rho_H + N_R \rho_R} \right) P$$

where        $\alpha$ = displacement/robotization tax rate
                  $N_R$ = number of robots in use in the firm
                  $N_H$ = number of humans in use at the firm
                          (employed or contracted)
                  $\rho_H$ = profit per human worker
                          (from industry stats)
                  $\rho_R$ = profit per robot in use ($\rho_R \sim 3\rho_H$)
                  $P$ = total annual profit of firm

Note:

- 100% of the profit of a fully robotized firm is subject to the tax.

- 0% of the profit of a firm using no robots is subject to the tax.

Example.

        $\rho_H$ = \$20,000 per human worker
        $\rho_R$ = \$60,000 per robot
        $\alpha$ = 1/3

$P = \$20,000,000$
$N_H = 60$
$N_R = 13$

$$\text{Tax} = \frac{1}{3}\left(\frac{13 \times \$60K}{60 \times \$20K + 13 \times \$60K}\right) \times \$20M$$
$$= \$2.63M$$

Assume no more than 25% of this is consumed by collection and enforcement costs.

This leaves 75% to support the 40 ($\sim 3N_R$) displaced human workers.

subsidy per displaced worker
$= (0.75 \times \$2.63M)/40 = \$49.3K$

**Were this tax imposed, would it still be profitable to replace human workers with robots?**

$$\text{Profit} = P = N_H \rho_H + N_R \rho_R$$
$$\text{Cost} = \text{tax} = \alpha\left(\frac{N_R \rho_R}{N_H \rho_H + N_R \rho_R}\right)\left(N_H \rho_H + N_R \rho_R\right)$$
$$= \alpha N_R \rho_R$$

Benefit = savings in worker costs
  = (humans replaced)(average human costs) −
    (robots)(robot costs)
  $= 3N_R C_H - N_R C_R$
  $= N_R(3C_H - C_R)$

$$\text{Benefit} - \text{Cost} = N_R(3C_H - C_R) - \alpha N_R \rho_R$$
$$= N_R(3C_H - C_R - \alpha \rho_R)$$

$$= N_R(3 \times \$50K - \$10K - 0.333 \times \$60K)$$
$$= N_R(\$120K) \leftarrow$$

where

$C_H = \$50K$ = (salary + payroll tax + benefits)
$C_R = \$10K$ = (repair + maintenance + lease)
$\alpha = 1/3$
$\rho_R = \$60K$

Yes. It easily pays to robotize if the cost of each replaced employee (salary + payroll tax + benefits) is a modest \$50K. It will likely pay for any employee cost above \$10K (i.e. whenever $C_H \geq \frac{1}{3}(C_R + \alpha \rho_R)$).

# Appendix 2

## The Fundamental Ethical Objective Stated Precisely

Suppose that a sentient creature accumulates happiness at some maximum rate when a desire is fulfilled, i.e. when the desire's intensity is reduced to zero. The total happiness over the foreseeable future is the sum for each desire of the happiness accumulated over this time. Occasionally, the intensity of a desire is reduced to zero as a consequence of the creature possessing it having died, been drugged, or rendered unconscious. Rather than counting this as a fulfilled desire, we shall remove it from the aforementioned sum. Hence, we have

$$h_i(t) = 1 - \frac{d_i(t)^2}{d_P^{\,2}} \tag{A.1}$$

$$H = \sum_{i=1}^{N} \int_{t_i}^{t_f} h_i(t)\varepsilon_i(t)\,dt \tag{A.2}$$

$$= \sum_{i=1}^{N} \int_{t_i}^{t_f} \left(1 - \frac{d_i(t)^2}{d_P^{\,2}}\right)\varepsilon_i(t)\,dt \tag{A.3}$$

where

$d_i(t)$ = intensity of the $i^{th}$ desire at time $t$

114

$d_P$ = intensity that a desire must have for its lack of fulfillment to be painful

$h_i(t)$ = rate of happiness accumulation for the $i^{th}$ desire at time $t$.

$H$ = total happiness accumulated over the foreseeable future

$t_i$ = initial time (at which moral actor contemplates action)

$t_f$ = final time (the end of the foreseeable future)

$\varepsilon_i(t)$ = 1 if the $i^{th}$ desire exists, *satisfied or not*, at time $t$
= 0 otherwise (desire not yet existing or terminated)

$N$ = total number of desires that exist at any time between $t_i$ and $t_f$

We may now define

*The Fundamental Ethical Objective – the maximization of H*

*The Fundamental Ethical Imperative – to maximally contribute to an increase in H, whenever one can act to increase it, and to minimally contribute to a decrease in H, otherwise.*

$H$ is obviously maximized by setting all desire intensities $d_i(t)$ to zero, i.e. by satisfying all desires. What is not readily apparent from (A.3) is that intensities of desires cannot be *freely* set to zero. They become zero only after the execution of desire-satisfying actions, which each involve a stupendous number of variables (describing the motion of all relevant particles) that are not shown.

We may further define

<u>terminated desire</u> – a desire whose intensity has been reduced to zero by some means other than its fulfillment.

<u>unterminated desire</u> – a desire that has not being terminated, i.e. one whose intensity is nonzero or whose intensity is zero due to its having been fulfilled.

<u>active desire</u> – an unterminated desire whose intensity is nonzero.

<u>fulfillable desire</u> – an active desire for which there exists a circumstance consistent with the laws of physics under which the desire's intensity would be zero.

<u>fulfilled desire</u> – an unterminated desire whose intensity is zero but can increase if circumstances change.

# Bibliography

REFERENCES

[1] "Cardinal Ratzinger Seeks a Bridge with Nonbelievers" December 12, 2004, Zenit.org [http://www.zenit.org/article-11791?l=English]

[2] "Cardinal Ratzinger on Europe's Crisis of Culture", July 29, 2005, Zenit.org [http://www.zenit.org/article-13705?l=English]

FURTHER READING

*Moral Machines – Teaching Robots Right from Wrong* by Wendell Wallach and Colin Allen (Oxford University Press, 2008)

*Beyond Human – Living with Robots and Cyborgs* by Gregory Benford and Elisabeth Malarte, (Forge Books, 2008)

*The Coming Robot Revolution – Expectations and Fears about Emerging Humanlike Machines* by Yoseph Bar-Cohen and David Hanson (Springer, 2009)

*Flesh and Machines – How Robots Will Change Us* by Rodney Brooks (Vintage, 2003)

*Wired for War – The Robotics Revolution and Conflict in the $21^{st}$ Century* by P. W. Singer (Penguin, 2009)

*Robo Sapiens – Evolution of a New Species* by
Peter Menzel and Faith D'Aluisio (MIT Press, 2000)

# ERRATA

www.eridanuspress.com/RobotNationErrata.html

www.ingramcontent.com/pod-product-compliance
Lightning Source LLC
Chambersburg PA
CBHW050529280326
41933CB00011B/1517